MAKERS WITH
A CAUSE

MAKERS WITH

A CAUSE

Creative Service Projects for Library Youth

Gina Seymour

LIBRARIES
UNLIMITED™

An Imprint of ABC-CLIO, LLC
Santa Barbara, California • Denver, Colorado

Copyright © 2018 by Gina Seymour

All rights reserved. No part of this publication may be reproduced, stored in a retrieval system, or transmitted, in any form or by any means, electronic, mechanical, photocopying, recording, or otherwise, except for the inclusion of brief quotations in a review, without prior permission in writing from the publisher.

Library of Congress Cataloging-in-Publication Data

Names: Seymour, Gina, author.
Title: Makers with a cause : creative service projects for library
    youth / Gina Seymour.
Description: Santa Barbara, California : Libraries Unlimited, [2018] |
    Includes bibliographical references and index.
Identifiers: LCCN 2018001638 (print) | LCCN 2018016307 (ebook) |
    ISBN 9781440857294 (ebook) | ISBN 9781440857287 (paperback)
Subjects: LCSH: Service learning. | Makerspaces in libraries. | School
    libraries—Activity programs.
Classification: LCC LC220.5 (ebook) | LCC LC220.5 .S49 2018 (print) |
    DDC 025.5—dc23
LC record available at https://lccn.loc.gov/2018001638

ISBN: 978-1-4408-5728-7 (paperback)
      978-1-4408-5729-4 (ebook)

22 21 20 19 18   1 2 3 4 5

This book is also available as an eBook.

Libraries Unlimited
An Imprint of ABC-CLIO, LLC

ABC-CLIO, LLC
130 Cremona Drive, P.O. Box 1911
Santa Barbara, California 93116–1911
www.abc-clio.com

This book is printed on acid-free paper ∞

Manufactured in the United States of America

The publisher has done its best to make sure the instructions and/or recipes in this book are correct. However, users should apply judgment and experience when preparing recipes, especially parents and teachers working with young people. The publisher accepts no responsibility for the outcome of any recipe included in this volume and assumes no liability for, and is released by readers from, any injury or damage resulting from the strict adherence to, or deviation from, the directions and/or recipes herein. The publisher is not responsible for any reader's specific health or allergy needs that may require medical supervision, nor for any adverse reactions to the recipes contained in this book. All yields are approximations.

For my husband Dr. Alan Seymour—without your love, help, support, and the endless cups of tea you made for me, this book would not have been possible. You make the world a better place through your dedication and compassion. I love you.

Contents

Introduction

Every child has it within himself or herself to make a difference in the world around them. As adult leaders and role models, we can help children develop empathy and compassion needed to effect this change. When it comes to making the world a better place, our young people are an untapped resource. Children are full of energy and passion, and when we help them channel these traits in positive directions, we all benefit. As professionals working with youth, we can encourage and engage young people in civic endeavors. Young people provide a unique voice as potential leaders for change. Our library youth are civically involved in causes that matter to them, and as library professionals and educators, we can help build upon the creativity and leadership of our youth. Young people view situations with fresh eyes and unique perspectives enabling them to successfully contribute to society.

Their skills can be expressed through compassion for others resulting in a real-world impact. There are many ways to address social needs. In this book, we'll focus on making tangible, useful handmade items. Awareness is the first step in bringing social change. As librarians and educators, we help youth learn about the world around them. You can't fix it if you don't know it's broken. Additional youth participants will get involved driven in the knowledge that they can do something to address a cause or situation when they see tangible contributions through meaningful action. These contributions to society have the ability to effect social change.

This book does not address face-to-face volunteering such as tutoring or service work at community agencies. This will look specifically at projects that can be made by youth to support a cause and not just by raising awareness. Focusing on project-based service, youth develop end products of benefit. Making encompasses all kinds of items, from coding to sewing. This book discusses a variety of maker activities from 3D printing to knitting and crocheting. Numerous service project ideas are presented, from simple low-cost, no-tech, craft-based ideas to high-tech projects, including 3D models.

Youth learn a great deal about dignity, humility, curiosity, compassion, and empathy through implementing the projects in this book. When using this guide, be sure to discuss with your youth group why the project is so important, how it helps, and whom it helps. Typically, service impacts the youth as a learner and, of course, the larger community. This reciprocal relationship provides for those in need and allows youth to discover more about the world around them and to develop problem-solving skills to impact these unfortunate situations. We all benefit.

"Makerspaces in the school library can serve as the perfect starting point for reimaging the very important space we occupy in the school" (Fleming 2015, 44). With this in mind, view your library through an innovative lens. Transformative making gives a unique sense of purpose to the space. Librarians can lead the way to empowering youth in our communities to be the change they wish to see.

An easy and popular MakerCare project benefiting shelter dogs.

In my school library, Islip High School, New York, we have a designated area of our makerspace dedicated to working on service projects. Our MakerCare program promotes and provides convenient service opportunities for our high school students. Students can use the area during the school day or after school, alleviating the need to find transportation to the point of service. Supplies and instructions are provided in one convenient location, accessible to all.

Young people carry out hands-on service projects, taking an active role in making a difference in their community and the world by creating purposeful items to be donated to various social agencies and charitable organizations. Our MakerCare initiative empowers students to make a difference, including how to build community partnerships and collaborate with staff. Young people develop academic and cognitive skills that build a culture of caring in the library makerspace and beyond.

Some students are required to perform service projects as part of their schooling or club membership. The librarian and the library makerspace can assist students in fulfilling those requirements, though "only 5 percent of youth attributed their volunteering activities to a school requirement" (Grimm, Dietz, Spring, Arey, and Foster-Bey 2005, 2). This book focuses on students in middle school and high school, though many projects, with or without modifications, can be used at the elementary level. Those who work on a variety of youth programs, teachers implementing service learning programs, and service-based club leaders will find this book useful.

In his book, *Free to Make*, Dale Dougherty states, "caring is in our toolbox." Let's take that a step further and load our toolbox not only with caring, but with compassion and empathy, too. Now add other supplies, things like glue, duct tape, and paint. Now mix them with innovation, determination, and grit. This toolbox will get us pretty far. In the scheme of things, these are the right tools for making a world of difference. So, as we begin our journey to making a difference, I ask you, "What's in your toolbox?"

HOW TO USE THIS BOOK

In the following pages, you will find easy-to-implement ideas and sage advice when developing a service program for youth in your library. This book is divided into two parts. This first part focuses on getting started and is divided into four chapters. The first chapter discusses the maker movement and youth service and their combined effect. The second chapter includes practical advice on setting up your makerspace work area. The third chapter of this part explains funding your maker-service projects, and finally, the fourth chapter covers building partnerships, strengthening collaboration, and effective communication. The second part focuses on service projects you can implement in your library program. The five chapters are broken down into the following themes: animal welfare; hunger, homelessness, and shelter; health and wellness; government and community-related service projects; and finally, service projects with global impact. The appendices include several communication templates, a list of calendar dates to assist program planning, and contact information for organizations mentioned.

Every day I have the honor and privilege of working with youth who are interested in making a difference in the world. I am compelled to share the lessons I've learned, complete with practical advice and simple instructions. My goal is that you will be successful when implementing service projects with youth. After you read this book, you will have a model for running a make-to-donate program serving library youth.

Together we can be the change!

Part I

GETTING STARTED

1

The Maker Movement, Service, and Today's Youth

In our democratic society, the library stands for hope,
for learning, for progress, for literacy,
for self-improvement and for civic engagement.
—Vartan Gregorian

MAKER MOVEMENT

Focused on science, technology, engineering, mathematics, and even the arts, the maker movement has taken center stage in recent years. The maker movement encourages tinkering, thinking, problem solving, collaboration, innovation, and creation. The maker movement recognizes makers of all ages. In fact, having attended numerous Maker Faires, notably the World Maker Faire in New York City, the National Maker Faire in Washington, D.C., and several Mini-Maker Faires in New York, the author believes youth participation is valued as much as adult and commercial participation at these venues. For these reasons, the maker movement has made its way into schools and libraries. This surge has made educational institutions searching for meaningful programs and projects.

In her book, *Worlds of Making*, Laura Fleming states that the ultimate outcome of educational makerspaces leads to "determination, independent and creative problem solving, and an authentic preparation for the real world by simulating real-world challenges" (2015, 48). Educators often think in terms of science, technology, engineering, and mathematics (STEM) and moreover applied mathematics, such as engineering and technology, when discussing makerspace activities. The predominance of maker activities focused on STEM prepares youth for real-world challenges in science-related job field. Youth can apply the same determination and problem-solving mind-set to any problem. So, what if we present youth with actual real-world challenges instead of school-based curriculum STEM challenges? With support, both by mentorship and by resources, young people are provided the opportunity to make a difference. What a perfect setup for helping the community and world! Think of a problem in your community, and then collaborate with a few friends to develop a solution. Through innovative thinking and collaborative problem-solving, youth create items to assist in making life better for others.

SERVICE

If you think about it, making isn't exactly a new idea. We've been doing it for centuries. For that matter, neither is compassion, a new concept, nor the willingness to serve. What is special is the ability and desire to bring these concepts together in a library maker-space. "Project-based service learning emphasizes educational opportunities that are inter-disciplinary, student-centered, collaborative, and integrated with real-world issues and practices. Students apply and integrate the content of different subject areas at authentic moments in the production process, instead of in isolation or in an artificial setting." Thus, "learning becomes relevant and useful as students establish connections to life outside of school. Authentic projects also help to address real-world concerns and develop real-world skills" (Bradford 2005, 29).

Service Projects versus Service Learning

Service learning is a curriculum-based learning process incorporating service to address community needs. Academic skills are assessed through community service projects using the National Youth Leadership Council's (NYLC) *K-12 Service-Learning Standards for Quality Practice*. Service learning standards include the following elements: meaningful service, link to curriculum, reflection, diversity, youth voice, partnerships, progress monitoring, and duration and intensity (NYLC 2009). While youth will use academic and social skills to create the community projects in this book, the emphasis is not on assessment and structured standards-based learning. The projects in this book can be used in any non-school library setting as the emphasis is not on formal educational learning or assessment, but solely on the youth's ability to create a meaningful outcome for the community. That is not to say that youth can and will be educated on the overall situation. Through awareness and need for items, educational learning will occur, albeit informally. This is still a powerful teaching moment in the lives of youth in that they discover they are capable of making change happen and can affect outcomes in their community and that they can work together to accomplish goals and change the world together using their talent, intellect, and passion. Our youth do not have to wait to "grow up" to solve a problem. Some of the examples discussed in this book originated from youth as young as six years old! We should encourage children to start early and continue throughout their lives.

One highly recommended aspect of traditional service learning is reflection. Guided reflection by the youth group instructor promotes a deeper understanding of issues of social justice, action, and outcome. Starting with awareness prior to beginning a project, we ask: why are we doing this? Who is affected? How does this make a difference? Youth then perform the service action and then are asked to reflect, with questions such as: How did you feel? What did you think while making this item or working on this project? Is this the best or only way to make a change? What else can or should be done? Youth then reflect on the process, the product, or the situation. Reflection allows participants to evaluate the experience and moves participants to the next level in learning and serving. Reflection nurtures insight, which in turn enables opinions to form. Upon reflection of the issue and examination of options, one can approach the issue with an effective problem-solving mind-set. We inspire and empower youth to act; ask them to reflect to complete the experience. For more on formal service learning, consult the NYLC.

Service to one's community is performed voluntarily and without remuneration. Service projects are implemented by volunteers to benefit others in the community or potentially worldwide and can include providing a service, such as volunteering time or an item, such as food for the homeless or a 3D printed prosthetic limb for a child. In the projects section of this book, you'll find instructions for actual items to be created and donated. Occasionally, these projects will be paired with additional service ideas making the overall service more constructive. For example, while making cat or dog toys for a local rescue group, run a food and supply collection, as well. Pairing both types of service adds to the overall benefit for the receiving agency. Overall, service projects focus on altruism and civic engagement without academic requirements.

Craftivism

Craft activists use crafting to influence policies and to challenge ideas and establishments with a desire to create social or political change often in the areas of "feminist and other civil rights movements, sustainability, and do-it-yourself [DIY] activities" (Garber 2013, 53). Some craftivists make large group items to bring awareness of a disease or cause. The creation of these crafts opens a dialogue where the viewer is inspired to ask questions. The crafted items are typically not used for a purpose other than promoting awareness, though sometimes items are raffled off to raise funds supporting a cause, such as the Priority Alzheimer's Quilt that raised funds for medical research. Another moniker bandied about is Crafting for a Cause. This involves crafting to draw attention to a situation that needs to be addressed more wholly. While craftivism is a worthwhile endeavor, the projects in this book are of a more functional nature; they are meant to be used. The items received are used by the recipients, as well as bring potential awareness to the cause. Yarn Bombing, a popular form of craftivism, is basically an art installation to bring attention to a cause or platform. This unique endeavor makes people stop, take notice, and ask questions. You can decide if this type of campaign is something your group would like to attempt. Yarn Bombing can also be used as an art installation to beautify your community. For more craftivist ideas and projects, read Betsy Greer's *Craftivism: The Art and Craft of Activism* (2014).

Making mixed with a social or political agendas is increasing. Depending on your group or situation, you may feel compelled to participate in this manner. However, one should be mindful of community standards set by your district and the age range of your youth. Librarians can be supportive of youths' individual convictions without promoting a specific agenda. Some of the projects in this book promote international peace and friendship, namely, the Peace Crane Project and the International Bookmark Exchange. Most projects listed in this book support humanitarian concerns; however, political messages and making have a potential of finding their way into your makerspace. A youth might use crochet time to make a "pussyhat," a popular Woman's March apparel representing support of women's rights, or perhaps use the arts supplies to create a political sign for an upcoming march or campaign. Group activities with political themes should be approached in an open and respectful manner. Our libraries are the "cornerstone of democracy in our communities" (American Library Association).

According to Dale Dougherty, "The Maker Movement asks us not only what technology can do but what good people can do as a community to use such tools to take care of ourselves and each other" (2016, 255). As librarians, we can help transform civic engagement. "By providing kids with opportunities to find out more about their communities and to become involved and make a difference in their communities, there is a chance that a new civic generation will emerge" (Durrance, Pettigrew, Jourdan, & Scheuerer 2001, 57).

According to the Corporation for National and Community Service (2007), youth stand to gain from service in three broad areas: academic engagement and achievement, civic attitudes and behavior, and social and personal skills.

RAKtivist

"RAKtivist" is short for "Random Acts of Kindness activist" and a registered trademark of the Random Acts of Kindness Foundation. Kids and youth leaders can sign up to be a RAKtivist. Lesson plans and ideas for promoting kindness and helping others are available online. Whether you sign up or form your own group, performing random acts of kindness promotes a more beautiful world.

Civic Engagement and Social Action

Our libraries "can play a valuable role in helping young children and teens better understand, become involved in, and make a contribution to their community. Programs that foster civic engagement among youth are making an investment in future citizen activism" (Durrance et al. 2001, 57). While developing work-related and soft skills, our youth become productive citizens in their community. Learning how to communicate, organize, prioritize, and plan is an essential college and career-ready skill. As mentors and role models, today's librarians are in an effective position to provide youth with assistance, supplies, and the community connections necessary to initiate change. Librarians are natural connectors, linking people with needs. As the youth-adult connector, we serve as the liaison between organizations and our young patrons. We empower our youth maker activist to learn responsible citizenship by having them take an active role in their community. Making a difference in the world can extend beyond our lifetime through fostering this generation. As role models, we have the power to nurture intrinsic motivation in youth. By viewing our passion for helping and making, youth will find and develop their own initiatives.

Maker activities can cultivate valuable learning opportunities among our youth. In our library makerspaces, students learn about science, technology, engineering, and even artistic expression. Yet there's a lot more that students can learn in a makerspace, namely, compassion and empathy. An effective way of promoting altruistic traits can be accomplished through making: not making for oneself but making to benefit others. Maker education doesn't have to be limited to STEM or STEAM but can embrace the whole child. Implementing a service program increases the scope of your makerspace or library programming through nurturing philanthropic qualities.

The Engineering Projects in Community Service (EPICS) program was started in 1995 for undergraduates at Purdue University and expanded to youth in high school in 2006. From there, the program quickly grew to include middle school students. EPICS is at the forefront encouraging youth to design and engineer real-world solutions to problems in their community from homelessness prevention to environmental protection to creating learning devices for children with disabilities (Purdue University). EPICS Club students in Illinois partnered with the MidAmerica Service Dog Foundation to design and create devices to benefit wheelchair-bound persons with guide dogs. Through creative planning and designing, students made a tennis ball thrower that attaches to a wheelchair making it possible for the recipient to interact with their guide dog companion. With this initial success, the club members plan "to design/engineer/build other devices to make the lives of service dog owners easier, like leash to collar connectors that can be fastened using large motor skills as opposed to fine" (Purdue University, "EPICS High School Examples").

DESIGN THINKING MIND-SETS AND PROCESS

Mind-Sets

There are many design thinking mind-sets to choose from; however, three worthy approaches are *learn by doing, think with your hands,* and *fail often* (Karalyte). All three are related and interconnected, so you can't do one without the other. Learn by doing allows us to get practical. Just thinking about problems or mulling over solutions is not enough to truly make a change. This leads us to the next critical mind-set, think with your hands. Youth can start with either a prototype or doodles on a page. Encourage them to use their hands to develop ideas and get what's in their brain out and in a physical representation. Finally, failure is necessary for success. So, embrace failure and know that you're that much closer to an actual solution. We learn by doing; we learn from our mistakes. Experiential learning is a vital process that embraces these three mind-sets.

Learning the Success of Failure

While we strive to protect children by intentionally setting them up for success to avoid the sadness of failure, we do our children a disservice, according to the book *The Gift of Failure*. Youth are deprived of the lessons failure provides such as "setbacks, mistakes, miscalculation, and failures that teach them how to be resourceful, persistent, innovative, and resilient citizens of this world" (Lahey 2015, xii). The word *failure* has an undo negative connotation. We all prefer smooth sailing and no roadblocks down each path we travel. But think about that for a moment. What if everything went smoothly? Young people would never learn about flexibility and adaptability, or grit for that matter. We owe it to youth to allow them to experience successful failures. Failure is a success in that learning, from the event, took place. From hands-on failure, youth can strengthen determination and grit. In her book *Grit: The Power of Passion and Perseverance*, Angela Duckworth (2016) states that grit can be learned and is a predictor of educational success. If so, don't we owe it to our youth to teach and model grit?

Empathy and the Empathic Mind-Set

Design thinking process is based on five stages: empathize, define, ideate, prototype, and test. The first step to design is empathy. We identify the user of the product or problem and then try to understand and identify his or her needs. Having empathy is the first step toward compassionate making and social action. "If we want to make a lasting impact on our students and prepare them to for success in college, career, and citizenship, we must prioritize empathy as an essential mindset" (Crowley & Saide 2016). And to this extent, it's not just enough to educate youth and encourage civic engagement, but allow and encourage youth to apply their academic knowledge and skills to transform their community, as well. "In the end, empathy will be the glue that effectively binds our knowledge and skills into a source for community growth" (Cress, Collier, & Reitenauer 2016, 16). During one of our maker sessions, students asked why we were making sleep mats for the homeless out of plarn (plastic grocery bags) instead of just buying sleeping bags. This was a very teachable moment as the student was questioned, "How would a person living on the street keep a fabric sleeping bag clean and free of bugs?" The students learned that plastic not only keeps one warm when on the cement, but also repels bugs. As for cleaning it, rinsing with water is all that's necessary for this lightweight alternative. Youth learned to analyze a situation and weigh the pros and cons of the assistance offered. The use of upcycled plastic also had a positive impact on the environment.

YOUTH

Young people are an available and untapped resource. Energetic, creative, and passionate about issues, today's youth can set the course for fixing numerous problems in their world. Youth can be successful with minimal assistance and mentoring. For the purpose of this book, we'll define youth as those in the 13–18-year-old age range, though many of the youth attributes and service project activities mentioned can be achieved with younger and older ages.

Our Influence on Youth

As educators and librarians, we are in a unique setting to influence young people not only elementary through high school, but throughout their lives. According to a Youth Services of America report, "Youth are most likely to volunteer because they are asked, and when they are asked, a teacher is the most likely person to make the request" (Spring, Dietz, & Grimm 2007, 2). Children need to practice compassion throughout youth development, and parents, educators, and youth community leaders can help as "volunteering is a learned social behavior, rather than an outcome of such characteristics as gender or race" (Grimm, Dietz, Spring, Arey, & Foster-Bey 2005, 14). We can engage youth in lifelong service as studies show "adults who began volunteering as youth are twice as likely to volunteer as adults as those who did not volunteer when they were younger" (Toppe, Golombek, Kirsch, Michel, & Weber 2002, 5). Our libraries "can play a valuable role in helping young children and teens better understand, become involved in, and make a contribution to their community. Programs that foster civic engagement among youth are making an investment in future citizen activism" (Durrance et al. 2001, 57). As educators, we can expose injustice while at the same time encourage youth to repair the world through service.

Academic and Social Benefits

Transformative, experiential learning teaches students "how to think critically about the world around them" and trains them "to become innovative citizens, people who see beyond surface causes and effect change in their communities and beyond" (Price-Mitchell 2015). An added benefit to community service is the "positive and statistically significant effect on scholastic progress" (Dávila & Mora 2007, 1). Through their research, Dávila and Mora further claim that "civic activities undertaken during high school are related to significantly higher odds that individuals graduate from college in later years" (2007, 3).

According to a survey of college students participating in academic service learning courses, there's a strong correlation between service participation and increased civic responsibility, as well as "the self-reported likelihood that students will continue to do volunteer work and will take an active role in helping address societal problems." And though a slightly weaker statistic, the survey also found a correlation between "life skills, including interpersonal skills and an understanding of people with a background different from one's own" (Gray, Ondaatje, & Zakaras 1999, 8–9). We owe it to future generations to instill a service mind-set in today's youth to, in turn, provide the next generation of civically responsible citizens determined to solve community problems both recurring and the ones that we have yet to experience.

Community service projects are a reciprocal learning/beneficial experience for both the youth and the community partner. There are many charitable organizations that need our help, and with simple supplies and guidance, we can empower youth to take an active role in making a difference in their community and, indeed, the world. Children experience empathy while strengthening their knowledge base. Both maker activities and service learning facilitate the acquisition of academic and cognitive skills. Many maker activities require math skills such as adding and measuring. Some require computer or writing skills. Critical thinking and authentic problem solving are just a few skills associated with this type of learning. Initiative, curiosity, leadership, persistence, and grit are "soft skills" learned by today's youth when actively and authentically engaged in solving problems. Most service projects require collaboration and communication. Youth learn how to do both while coping with setbacks and forging ahead with their civic mission. However, some of the ultimate skills students learn are compassion, kindness, and concern for their community and for their fellow humans through active citizenship. Promoting civic engagement among our students has lasting effects.

The benefits of learning a crafting skill such as sewing or crocheting provides youth with potentially employable skills such as tailoring or lifelong hobby. Sewing requires authentic application of arithmetic—measuring, ratios, and fractions are par for the course. Overall, volunteers are happier and do better academically in school (DoSomething.org 2012).

Characteristics of Youth Volunteers

DoSomething.org is one of the largest youth-centered organizations aimed at social action. Its research is a comprehensive survey analyzing youth volunteers and will allow you to consider who your potential volunteers are and how to design service initiatives geared to their needs. Based on *The DoSomething.org Index on Young People and Volunteering* survey analysis, the following suggestions will help you set up a youth service program in either a school or a public library (2012, 29).

Young people see volunteering as a social event and want to work with friends. They need accessibility when volunteering, preferring a place close to home where no car is necessary, but they don't want work at home. Young people are looking for brief or singular time commitments. Projects that allow youth to come and go as they please or those that allow for short levels of engagement are desirable. This is a perfect scenario for a school or public library program. Both are local community based and typically easy to access. Friends of participants are encouraged to join the group making the social aspect easy to maintain. Youth tend to volunteer intermittently and in informal ways. Having a drop-in maker station is beneficial for attracting youth by catering to convenience for participation. Schools and public libraries are familiar and used to youth coming and going attending programs periodically. Libraries as hubs of the community or school welcome groups of youth through regular programming. Libraries and service-oriented teens are a perfect fit. Ever wondered how to increase youth participation in your library programming? It's simple, look to the research and analyze which youth and why they want to participate in service. Then tailor your program to meet their needs. Use the characteristics listed earlier to design your program. Issues that teens care about are animal welfare, hunger, and homelessness; all three topics are covered in this book (DoSomething.org 2012, 15).

Disadvantaged Youth

"Young people from low-wealth families often don't volunteer because they aren't asked, don't have the resources, or aren't offered opportunities that will improve their own community" (DoSomething.org 2012, 17). When asked to volunteer, "a teacher is the most likely person to make the request" (Spring et al., 2007, 2). Most teens want to volunteer to help others and not because it "looks good on a resume" (Parker & Franco 1999, 171; Grimm et al. 2005). Disadvantaged youth are significantly more motivated by the prospect of gaining work experience than their non-disadvantaged peers, but when volunteering, they show the same level of commitment as non-disadvantaged peers (Spring et al. 2007, 2). Research shows disengaged youth are less likely to engage in risky behaviors when quality volunteer opportunities are introduced (Grimm et al. 2005). Highly proficient at programming and promotion, librarians can address and plan inclusive activities for youth, whether in a school or public library. Libraries in low-income areas can run a maker service program even with limited budgets. (See Chapter 3 for funding ideas.)

As in many communities, we have a mix of income levels. All youth should be invited and encouraged to participate in community service and goodwill activities. Host a "*Make the Holidays Special*" event where students can come to the makerspace and create holiday gifts for giving. It's not specifically for youth who cannot afford to buy gifts, but those with limited funds benefit by feeling "normal" in the frenzy of gift-giving season: Perler bead craft or bracelet for a friend, photo frame or ornament for mom and dad. You'll be very busy just before a gift-giving holiday such as Christmas, Hanukkah, or Kwanzaa. Run a fragrant bath salt craft for Mother's Day. Recipients appreciate the handmade gifts and cards over the generic, costly mall purchase. Programming such as this does not single out students of low socioeconomic status, as all students are welcome and all are active participants; there's no stigma. Youth become accustomed to making for others. Disadvantaged youth who volunteer benefit from increased self-esteem, skills, and academics (Spring et al. 2007, 4). At-risk students state service "gave them a sense of importance, self-confidence, and responsibility that they didn't feel they had before" (Nelson & Eckstein 2008, 231). With the right programming, all youth can participate and benefit.

Youth with Special Needs and Inclusive Volunteering

By participating in positive, enriching experiences, English language learners (ELLs) and students with disabilities (SWDs) can benefit from service programs. Students benefit from the real-world experiences while developing academic and social skills. Often the recipients of services, youth with special needs are not frequently viewed as potential volunteers. Students with disabilities experience "improved self-esteem, sense of purpose, social connectedness, happiness, quality of life and community inclusion" when volunteering (Miller, Schleien, Brooke, Frisoli, & Brooks 2005, 18). With this in mind, strive to be more inclusive as the benefits are so impactful. Additional benefit noted "included pride, skill development and generalization, empowerment, and increases in social interaction and verbal communication" (Miller, Schleien, Rider, Hall, Roche, & Worsley 2002, 247).

ELLs get to feel part of the overall school community and begin participating in civic engagement in their new country. Working together with non-ELL peers and native speakers provides non-native speakers increased opportunities to acquire language skills, in addition to hands-on and cognitive skills. An organization such as PostCard Pick Me Up allows non-native English speakers to write and decorate postcards to hospitalized patients in languages other than English. There are patients in hospitals who, like ELLs, do not read or speak English well. This is a nice entry to service for new immigrants who have limited to no English language proficiency. More proficient ELLs can practice their writing skills in English. And creative, artistic decorative designs on the backs of the postcards transcend language. Our youth regardless of English language proficiency can also be positive change-makers in their communities. Service makes ELLs feel more connected and accepted at school and within the community, while reinforcing language skills through meaningful authentic experiences (Russell 2007).

Including ELLs in all activities helps them feel part of the larger community. Working side by side provides an opportunity for ELLs to interact socially with their non-ELL peers. The importance of "programs that allow ELL students to learn as equals alongside English-speaking peers, in ways that value the skills and abilities of everyone" (Kilman, 2009, 17) is highly beneficial on many levels because it enables students to "feel . . . . community" (Kilman, 2009, 19). For ELLs, service is not just about academics and skill building; "it also teaches them to reach out to others, to take pride in and ownership of their community, and to learn and improve as human beings" (Russell 2007, 771). Many of the projects in this book include guidelines for making the activity inclusive for limited language proficiency participants.

Every young person should have an opportunity to change the world with no one left out. "By modeling the citizenship we want students to embody we can create the culture and climate that validates all, excludes none" (Crowley & Saide 2016). Making encompasses all abilities and all languages and benefits all student populations. Youth with disabilities benefit from self-esteem and sense of empowerment, increased social interaction, and skills development (Miller et al. 2002, 247). Do not withhold information about service opportunities or limit participation in service activities. "Information about service activities must be made accessible to all students, not just those deemed 'leaders' by school personnel" (Parker & Franco 1999, 174). Making a difference should not be exclusive, but rather inclusive.

2

Makerspace Setup

When you make something with your hands, it changes the way you feel,
which changes the way you think, which changes the way you act.
—Carl Wilkens

Physical space does not solely define the importance of a makerspace. Makerspaces enable making by providing space, tools, materials, and mentors. Makerspaces bring together individuals with varying interests to work individually or collaboratively to explore interests. It is not necessary to have a large makerspace with costly supplies; a simple setup is all that is required. There are large makerspaces with expensive gadgets and gizmos aplenty and smaller pop-up makerspaces outfitted with a multidrawer plastic cart on wheels. It's all good, for the most important thing needed are youth who want to make a difference in their community and world. There is no "one-size-fits-all" model for makers or makerspaces. Each library site is unique, and one needs to assess the situation at hand to make the most of available resources.

PHYSICAL SPACE ASSESSMENT

Look around your space and consider your needs. Do you have space for your teens to work, or do you need to use a shared space such as a community room? Is storage space available for your supplies available? Are there electrical outlets you can plug into? How many and how close are they to your worktable? Do you have access to a sink for cleanup? If not, where is the nearest one? While these are critical questions, they do not limit the function of your group participation if not available. There are always alternatives. If a sink is not readily available, consider the purchase of baby wipes and paper towels for cleanup and to keep messes in check as you work. Of course, for a thorough cleanup, access to cleaning supplies and a bathroom or kitchen sink is essential. Don't have access to outlets? Battery-operated glue guns and other tools are available for purchase. Do not get discouraged for a lack of resources; instead brainstorm alternatives. A dedicated makerspace is optimal but not exclusively necessary. It is more convenient for staff to have a workspace and supplies in one spot, but there will always be limitations in physical work space and so adapt accordingly. You'll need storage space and storage containers for your supplies—at least one large sturdy table as a worktop. If working with a large group of teens simultaneously, multiple sturdy tables are needed. If space is available in your library, set aside an area or table so youth can work on service projects throughout the day. This is a convenience and an encouragement for individual and small-group participation. When working with large groups, physical space between participants is necessary particularly when working with tools, specifically power tools, hot glue guns, or irons. Keep this in mind when planning a session. Safety is paramount.

SAFETY

In addition to considering space between participants, clear communication when using electrical devices, such as glue guns, power tools, or soldering irons, is imperative. Instruction on their use and safety when items are not in use needs to be communicated to participants prior to their use. When necessary, have safety devices such as goggles available for each participant. Be mindful of power cords as a tripping hazard and burns caused by glue guns. When working with children, always stress the importance of safety and be sure to model said behavior as well.

Here are some basic common-sense guidelines:

- Shut off and put away items that are not in use. If you don't need it on your worktable, put it away.
- Clean up messes as they occur. Actually, it's best to just clean up everything as you go along. Baby wipes and paper towels are handy to have around for this purpose.
- Participants should be aware of their surroundings and of others. School bags should be set aside to limit tripping hazards.
- In case of an accident, participants should notify the librarian and/or call 911 immediately.

Keep in mind, you are working with youth who need you to teach, guide, and model safe, appropriate behavior.

TYPES OF MAKERSPACES

Mobile Makerspaces

Do you need a dedicated makerspace? Let's just say it's nice to have all supplies at the ready in one spot, but a program can certainly run almost anywhere. Our local public library has a "maker cart" that is loaded with supplies and is available to teens upon request. They run a few service-oriented activities each quarter, as well. We occasionally collaborate to work on the same projects at around the same time. Kids can use the public library's mobile maker cart on the weekend and evenings, and they can use our dedicated makerspace at school. We both provide a similar service regardless of our individual space issues. Mobile carts, as the name implies, are versatile in that they can be moved to wherever you desire. Your supplies are in one spot, but mobile: beneficial for both school and public library settings without the space to dedicate a specific maker area or for those programs that want or need flexibility. Mobile makerspaces can be carts or rolling storage trunks or bins. Both provide functional storage space for supplies and portability. You may have one storage trunk large enough for your supplies, or you may need several. Carts and bins can be arranged by project types: one bin for sewing materials, another for drawing, and yet another for 3D printing supplies. Just pull out the bin you need for your group at the time you need it. These mobile makerspaces can be wheeled out as needed for programming or individuals. Your program may grow, and you may decide to convert a little-used space in your library or perhaps your library undergoes renovations allowing you a dedicated makerspace. Don't worry, the mobile carts won't go to waste as they are still good storage options. And keep in mind, as your program grows, so will your storage needs.

Makerspace on the Go/Pop-Up Makerspaces

At the 28th Annual National Service Learning Conference "Dare to Dream" in Anaheim, California, in addition to plenary sessions and workshops, the conference hosted on-site service opportunities in the exhibit hall. During the three-day conference, participants had a convenient opportunity to make a difference locally and globally. Conference attendees stuffed dolls, made animal toys for local shelters, and helped save the oceans by upcycling plastic bags into jump ropes. All items were collected and donated to various local agencies. This took quite a bit of planning, but with so many willing participants, short work was made of the tasks. So many maker activities can be done outdoors or down the block, so don't overlook this great outreach opportunity. You just need to plan, pack, and wheel.

STORAGE OPTIONS

As noted earlier, mobile carts and mobile plastic bins provide good storage options. Book shelving from a decreasing print reference collection can transform into a storage or project display area. Libraries buying more digital resources versus print leave prime real estate for the taking. You'll find your storage needs increase in tandem with your program and participation; capitalize on any underused space in your library. The use of recycled cardboard boxes for item storage is a low-budget alternative; however, you may find the use of clear plastic storage bins preferable. Clear bins allow you to see what's inside quickly and perform a quick check on supply levels, as well.

What needs to be locked up? Soldering irons, fabric scissors, x-acto knives, and box cutters are items best kept aside until needed. With safety in mind, don't leave these specific supplies out not knowing if your teens know how to use them. Many youth who need or use these items need little supervision. However, you may have newbies in need of a bit of instruction and supervision prior to being set free. Try to know the maturity and skill level of your youth group and gauge the appropriate supervision necessary. Older students with experience require less supervision than tweens with limited skill. Additional adult supervision may be necessary.

BASIC SUPPLIES

Keep in mind makerspaces are not in the "one-size-fits-all" category. Your group's age, skills, and choice of activities will determine your maker supply needs. Some of these items you may have on hand already and others you may be fortunate enough to acquire through donations. Always ask for donations, as it frees up funds for other supplies and projects. A basic list of supplies:

Crayons in a variety of colors
Markers in a variety of colors
Colored pencils in a variety of colors
Construction paper in a variety of colors
Washable paint in a variety of colors
Paintbrushes

White school glue
Craft glue (such as Mod Podge)
Glue sticks
Glue gun
Cellophane tape
Book tape
Masking tape
Duct tape
Ribbon in a variety of colors
Yarn in a variety of colors
Scissors
Fabric in a variety of colors

Supplies for many of the activities in this book can be obtained through donations or up-cycling. Seek out these projects if your budget is limited or nonexistent. Every makerspace needs certain basic supplies such as scissors, glue, and drawing paraphernalia. Even within these categories, there are options. In the following section are guidelines and caveats to assist you when selecting the tools and supplies you will need.

Scissors

Basic all-purpose scissors are a must. Ideally one scissor should be available for each participant; however, for some activities, supplies can be shared or teams can work on separate components of the activity, lessening the need for one-to-one supplies. When selecting shears, choose an ambidextrous model or better still have several pairs of left-handed shears available to accommodate all. Most average scissors are designed for right-handers. Left-handed youth are frustrated and hindered by tools detrimental to their abilities. Choose an eight-inch blade size for teens. Five-inch models are better suited for young children with smaller hands. In addition to multipurpose scissors, an investment in fabric scissors is highly beneficial. If you can't afford fabric scissors, let your community know you'll accept donations. All our fabric scissors and pinking shears were acquired from a local family whose mother, a seamstress, passed away. The family contacted the school to inquire if her collection could be used. We received not only these costly professional tools but also quality fabrics and her button collection. Many projects require fabric, and having dedicated fabric scissors makes the work of cutting much easier. Always spread the word for the kinds of supplies you'd like to receive through word of mouth or social media. There will be more on this in subsequent chapters on funding and partnerships. Remember to keep your fabric scissors in a dedicated secure area, as using these scissors on anything other than fabric will ruin them. Many youths will be tempted to reach for the closest pair of scissors on a table, but expensive, good-quality fabric scissors should only be used for cutting fabric or thread. Youth need to be apprised of this, as it won't be self-evident to them. They need you to educate them, and consistent reminders are essential. Store your fabric scissors separately.

Glues

You'll need all-purpose white glue and glue sticks. These are inexpensive, but consumable so you'll need a constant supply. Mod Podge is a basic crafting glue that dries clear and is easy to clean up with soap and water. Mod Podge is a combined glue and sealer that comes in various finishes such as matte and gloss and works on various surfaces. Glue guns come in hot and cool temperature, or you can buy dual temperature glue guns. When purchasing glue guns, don't forget to consider access to electrical outlets. You may also need power strips or multiple outlet extension cords based on your physical layout and access to electrical outlets to accommodate the use of multiple glue guns. Consider space and safety. Some models are cordless allowing for flexibility and movement. It might be beneficial to keep youth tethered if you feel unsafe with them walking around with hot glue. If you don't have access to electricity, battery-operated glue guns are available. Keep in mind if you purchase battery-operated models, you'll have to budget for batteries, too.

Paper

Basic 8 × 11½ white printer paper, construction paper, and cardstock paper weight (20 lb and higher) all in varying colors will cover most basic projects. Decorative origami paper comes in handy as well. You may wish to collect recycled, used greeting cards or left-over wrapping paper. These are free and could come in handy. Recycle promotional address labels by cutting off the address section, keeping only the cute sticker designs. Use these stickers to dress up postcards for sick children and other projects.

Specialty Items
Textiles

Have a selection of ribbons and fabrics on hand. Here's where you may get lucky and receive donations of leftover pieces and yards from a local crafter's project. Most of the projects in this book can be accomplished with a yard or less of fabric. Therefore, scraps and leftovers received for free or purchased for a nominal fee, such as remnants, are perfect. You'll need needles and assorted cotton thread. Black and white threads are a must—all other colors are acquired as needed, preferred, or donated.

Sewing Machines

It is nice to have, but you must also consider maintenance and storage of these items. Our sewing machines were acquired by digging around the school basement. Not the best storage option for these machines, so in a sense I was liberating them! If your budget precludes the purchase of these items, partner with a community sewing club, often formed and meeting at public libraries, or if you're in a school, collaborate with your Family and Consumer Science department's sewing teacher. Community members with the requisite skill set willing to work with your group is another option. These maker-mentors are highly beneficial to any program. Remember, if you don't have the essential skills, form a partnership with someone who does. If your budget allows, a basic model with minimal features is your best option for both ease of use and maintenance, and cost-effectiveness. If you need several, purchase all the same make and model machines. This will save time in giving instructions and fixing problems, as multiple models can lead to frustration and time-consuming fixes.

3D Printers

Don't run out and purchase a 3D printer for your entry into service projects or even making. However, if you happen to have one in your library or are able to borrow one through a library consortium-sharing program, there are projects that provide a service. Most of the service projects listed in this book do not require a 3D printer.

Creating prosthetic limbs in partnership with the Enabling the Future group is one example of a 3D printing project found in this book. This group encourages individuals to use their 3D printers to create free 3D printed hands and arms for those in need of these assistive devices. Students at Summit Christian Academy in Cedar Park, Texas, went a step further by using their 3D printer and to print a prosthetic hand for a classmate born without a left hand (Kravets 2017). So sometimes lending a helping hand can strike close to home.

While having a dedicated makerspace available is convenient, it is not essential. Many of the examples listed can be achieved in a typical classroom, library setting, or community center. The only truly indispensable element needed is a good heart, along with a work area and basic supplies like scissors and glue. Inside this book are a few ideas to get started on your journey to create a culture of caring in your library. Just remember the most important tool you have is your hands. With your hands, creative thinking, determination, and a few supplies see us well stocked to make a difference.

3

Funding Your Service Projects

Service to others is the rent you pay for your room here on earth.
—Mohammed Ali

So you have good intentions, willing youth, and a place to work, but how are you going to fund this endeavor? Best advice—start simple and stay local. Projects with few materials, preferably using upcycled items donated locally, are a perfect way to begin. Braided dog toys made from donated upcycled T-shirts and donated to a local animal shelter or rescue group are a simple and no-cost way to make a difference in your community. Search for civic organizations, societies, and religious groups in your area that are willing to provide funds and resources if you provide the youth volunteers.

THE SUSTAINABILITY MOVEMENT AND UPCYCLING

Many items end up in our landfills that could otherwise serve an additional purpose, and these discards have a negative impact on the environment. Upcycle by converting old or discarded materials into something useful. Every item produced has an environmental impact. From production to transport, energy and water resources are being used. Reusing materials reduces our ecological footprint, having a positive impact on the environment by removing items from the global garbage accumulation. Sleep mats for the homeless made from plastic grocery bags are virtually free to make. All that is needed are volunteers to collect bags, cut the bags into strips, and connect the strips into one continuous string forming plarn (plastic yarn). Crochet the plarn into mats. One mat removes 500 to 700 plastic bags from our landfills. Some states and local communities are discontinuing the use of plastic grocery bags. This is a good thing, but it does not remove all the plastic bags from our environment. We still have many plastic bags in our daily lives, such as dry cleaner plastic cloth covers and newspaper delivery sleeves. Upcycle these items for projects, too. They're free and you have an endless supply. Upcycle mailing address labels received from charities. Just cut off the addresses, and you have really cute stickers for free. These stickers can be used for a variety of projects, including decorating postcards for hospitalized children. Upcycled items to always have on hand include cereal boxes, jars and cans, fabric, and T-shirts. Last week's newspapers are great for protecting tables. And who knows, maybe you'll find a hidden message from your youth participants.

Youth expressing themselves. Message discovered after a volunteer session.

Each project in this book lists the materials needed and any potential for upcycling. This is done not only to protect the planet and its resources, but is a great way to save money. You need funds to start or replenish your programming supplies of consumable products such as glue sticks and colored markers. The less outlay of funds stretches your budget and allows for the development and implementation of additional programs. Even if you are fortunate to have a robust budget, do the world a favor and upcycle.

DONATIONS

Typically, donations come from two sources: individuals and businesses. Review librarian and educator groups on social media sites for information about companies giving away free supplies and promotions. Your personal learning network is a fountain of information with free and low-cost promotional opportunities shared through social media. Join popular education and crafting groups on Facebook. The Yarn Council (www.craftyarn council.com/) occasionally gives away free kits of yarn and crochet hooks, and word of mouth spreads quickly on social media. Receiving a box of 20 skeins of yarn and hooks allows you to create some of the projects in the back of this book. Yarn, crochet hooks, and knitting needles are easily donated by individuals in your community. Many crafters welcome the chance to share their overabundant stock. Before beginning a project, look at the supply list and mentally match potential donors. Whom can you ask for donations? Consider local businesses, chain stores, or members of your community. Tap into local residents who support your endeavors. They are "go-to" people when looking for donations, whether purchased or upcycled. Keep them up to date on your program needs. These people keep your program moving forward and your budget in check.

Set up donation bins in the library to collect items needed for projects. Two benefits are: there's a place for donations as they arrive, and the designated area brings attention to the work you're doing and the items you need. It starts a conversation and serves as a visual marketing tool. With this free publicity, you'll receive more donations.

However, there will be times when you'll think, *that's not quite the donation I requested* or someone's interpretation of *gently used* differs from yours. Not to worry. For the most part, accept all donations graciously as something can usually be done with them, for example, T-shirt donations; there are so many projects that can be made out of them. So many upcycled projects such as a no-sew bag or scarf are perfect for craft fair fund-raisers.

Bins advertise upcoming projects.

For those projects, you'll want better quality T-shirts. But what to do with some of the shabby, stained donations you receive? Cut them up into strips and braid them into dog toys for local dog rescue groups. One donation supply drive—multiple options. When we request pillowcases for the Little Dresses for Africa project, the receipt of unflattering pillowcases is not a concern, as I know they can be donated to our town animal shelter. The shelter workers need pillowcases when going out on calls to retrieve loose snakes in the neighborhood. See, problem solved and everyone benefits. How do you find out about the needs of your town animal shelter? Communication. The more you interact with your community partners, the more you'll learn about their specific operational needs, not just the obvious ones. Store this information away for when it's needed.

SHOW ME THE MONEY

Grants

A grant is a set sum of money that is given to the recipient after an application process. Most grants are for specific causes, so you'll have to find one that matches your project's needs. Also, all grants have a specific set of requirements. Don't apply if you don't meet those requirements. Grants are not guaranteed and are typically a onetime funding source. Though some grants can carry over into years, they are not typical. Grants are available from educational foundations, private foundations, corporations, and the government.

Here are some places to look for grants:

- Do Something—DoSomething.org/grants
- Youth Service America—ysa.org/grants

- The FreeChild Project—freechild.org/funds4progress.htm
- Ashokas Changemakers—changemakers.com/opportunities
- Awesome Foundation—www.awesomefoundation.org/en where micro-grants of $1,000 are given out on a monthly basis.
- Diana Rendina has an extensive list of grant resources on her website, *Renovated Learning*. Look in the resources tab for the Grants & Funding link. http://renovatedlearning.com/grant-resources/.

These are some of the larger organizations out there offering grants. Don't overlook community-based groups such as Kiwanis, Rotary or Lions Club, as they are excellent funding sources. As community members themselves, they want you to succeed in making the community better. National craft stores, such as JoAnne's and AC Moore, have funding opportunities for nonprofits and educators. Search your local chain craft store's website for possible funding.

Crowdfunding

Use a crowdfunding platform to appeal directly to the public for funds. There are generous people in your community and elsewhere who would like to directly support your efforts. Crowdfunding is the practice of direct funding of projects by individuals, unlike grants which are given by organizations. Monetary contributions by individual donors can be solicited online. Crowdfunding platforms, such as Donors Choose, Pledge Cents, and GoFundMe, are Internet based.

Donors Choose (www.donorschoose.org/)—Citizen donors along with corporate and foundation partners provide educators with funding. This is school based for educators. The process is simple; submit an online summary of your project and financial needs. Your project needs to be approved by Donors Choose reviewers. You must meet your goal funding, if not you don't get to keep the funds.

GoFundMe (https://www.gofundme.com/)—You don't need to be a school or nonprofit; anyone can set up a campaign on this social fund-raising platform. There are no deadlines or goal requirements. You're not penalized for missing a goal; you get to keep all the money you receive, unlike platforms such as Donors Choose. You can submit any project; it does not need to be approved. GoFundMe does not charge fees to your donors. The funds you receive have a standard processing fee deducted; most sites charge about 3 percent. You'll have additional fees to use the website platform. GoFundMe charges around 5 percent. Therefore, in this scenario, the monies you raise will be given to you minus approximately 8 percent.

Pledge Cents (https://www.pledgecents.com/)—Similar to GoFundMe in that you get to keep the funds raised even if you don't meet your goal. They focus solely on PreK–12 education; referred to as the "GoFundMe for classrooms." They take 5 to 8 percent of money raises, same as GoFundMe.

Service-Based Crowdfunding

Start Some Good (https://startsomegood.com/)—Crowdfunding platform for social impact projects. Projects need to reach full funding goal to receive payment. Standard processing fees of approximately 8 percent apply; 5 percent applied to Start Some Good; and 3 percent to cover the credit card processing agent, Stripe.

Generosity by IndieGoGo (www.generosity.com/)—Run by the popular crowdfunding site IndieGoGo, Generosity is focused on social-minded fund-raising. Generosity does not charge any fees, but you will need a payment processor, Stripe account. It charges 3 percent. Regardless of meeting your funding goal, you'll receive all funds collected.

Piggybackr (www.piggybackr.com/)—Fees total approximately 7 percent, with 4 percent going to Piggbackr and 3 percent going to payment processing. You can collect funds regardless of reaching your funding goals provided you collect a minimum of $50.

Fund-Raisers

Some service-based youth groups host traditional bake sales or run a car wash to raise funds. This is one way to go; however, you need to recognize the time, and energy expended might be better served elsewhere. One exception is a craft sale that displays some of the products created by your teens. This is a great way to advertise your group's mission and gain some new supporters. Focus more on upcycled products so you raise more money with less outlay of funds. See the introduction to the projects section for more ideas and details on hosting fund-raising events.

Budgets

Some of us have a budget for library-related materials and programs. You may be able to tap into some of your funds, but many libraries may find it challenging to provide even basic resources to their patrons. Purchase orders may be required by your institution, and W-9s and Sole Source vendor letters may also be required for unique purchases. If a service or item is only available from one vendor, your organization may require a Sole Source letter stating the item is only available through this source. Some organizations require three vendor quotes or the use of only state-approved vendors. Familiarize yourself with the purchasing requirements of your institution.

Sponsorships

Requesting a sponsor or offering sponsorships for your program or a specific project is another option for seeking needed funds. Ask a company, or individual, to financially sponsor your endeavor, and in return they receive recognition and publicity. Recognition and publicity is unusually handled through your website, blog, tweets, or other social media. This is a mutually beneficial scenario, as you receive needed funds, and your sponsor receives a potential tax write-off and community-wide goodwill publicity.

WAYS TO SAVE MONEY AND SPEND LESS

Discounts

Many chain craft stores offer discounts for educator purchases. Regardless of whether you're in chain stores or local mom-and-pop shops, ask for a discount! At worst they'll say no and you're no worse off than when you first arrived. Best-case scenario, you'll get a discount or occasionally free stuff, too. Always ask. And don't forget those coupons! Always look at the clearance section of craft stores and elsewhere. Many bargains can be had in the clearance bin at your local chain craft store. Make friends with the managers of the stores you frequent. They will call or text you regarding items about to go on clearance. Hundreds of dollars can be saved through the goodwill and advanced notice of store managers. As community members, store managers get to know you and your program and they want to help.

Borrow

A 3D printer may be available at your school. Even if it's not in your library, you can most likely use it with permission. Additionally, county library systems and school cooperative systems are now lending out 3D printers to schools and public libraries. Resources can be shared through lending programs, among library systems or departments. Consortium sharing allows you to try out different products on the market and allows you to determine which features you value when getting ready to make a similar purchase. This ability to try out expensive equipment prior to making a potential costly mistake is extremely beneficial and fiscally smart. You might not be able to budget for a high-ticket item, but chances are you could borrow one.

Surplus Items

Is there a surplus supply warehouse in your area? Not sure? Check out the Public Surplus website (www.publicsurplus.com), a national database of public agencies who are divesting themselves of unwanted items. One person's excess is another's treasure. Search for other warehouse supply programs in your area. In New York City, Materials for the Arts collects donations from businesses and individuals and then gives away these supplies free to nonprofit organizations with arts programming, government agencies, and public schools in the area. Surplus items can also be found online on Craig's List. Listed are classified ads getting rid of items like Public Surplus; however, instead of dealing with public agencies, you are dealing directly with individuals. Some are not comfortable with meeting a stranger to pick up a donation, but safe situations can be arranged. If you're fine with this scenario, you'll score lots of treasures.

But why travel to pick up items? Have you visited the basement of the school or library where you work? You'll be surprised at how much is available for the taking. Of course, ask your supervisor first if you may visit (aka pilfer). This is your first stop to finding treasures such as storage cabinets, work tables, and in my case, sewing machines from a discontinued course. Just remember: *Beg, Borrow, and Steal*—ask for discounts and free stuff, borrow from others including consortiums in your area, and feel free to raid the basement or attic of your library building!

The Retired, the Moving, and the Dead

From these three categories, you can gain copious supplies. Know someone retiring? Moving? Kids off to college? All good reasons to clear out offices, closets, basements, and garages. Each year schools and libraries announce the new retirees, and they are happy to divest themselves of 30 years' worth of stuff. Be sure to let them know how their contributions will continue to help others. Offering donors a book cart and youth to help move items from their office or car is not only very practical, but it usually results in larger than expected donations. You're offering them convenience and the ability to continue to help others. In addition to the retirees, there are others in your organization moving to downsize from house to condo divesting themselves of countless items in the process. With limited space, supplies from a side business or personal hobby are donated to your program as they won't fit in the new downsized abode. Donors avoid time-consuming yard sales and managing eBay listings and, in the process, provide your program with good quality and often unaffordable supplies.

Maker programs can benefit from deceased community members when family members recognize your program can benefit more from the donation rather than having a yard sale. Knowing that youth benefit and the feeling of giving to the community are significant motivators. When you publicly thank residents for their donations, others in the community become aware of your needs and more donations will turn up on your doorstep. The best yard sale finds are from estate sales. Families don't share grandma's enthusiasm for sewing, knitting, or crafting and want to clean out the house as soon as possible for sale. Explain what you do and the impact your program has, and then make an offer for everything or boxes at a time. The family doesn't have to deal with selling each item individually and the potential of getting stuck with leftover items. In this scenario, you walk away with a cache. Even if you don't know what's at the bottom of the box, the family may be eager to get rid of everything with you acquiring hidden treasures.

Fabrics, knitting and crochet hooks, if not acquired by donations, are easily found at yard sales and thrift stores. Be sure to tell people what you do and whom you help; you might just gain a larger discount or donation than you anticipated.

Social Media

Leverage social media to not only recruit volunteers and advertise your good works, but to also acquire donations. When posting to social media:

- *Target others who can help.* Tag organizations and community leaders who can help your mission. Not only can these people potentially help, but they can also help you get your message out to their followers by sharing or retweeting.
- *Be specific. What* do you need? *When* do you need it by? *Where* is the drop off location? *Who* to speak to if there are further questions? Always include contact information as these conversations often lead to new opportunities, further funding, or helpful new contacts. You may want to include *why* you need it. You'll often see and hear responses from people stating they chose to help because the project reminded them of their beloved aunt or a special childhood memory. Humanize the request for greater response and participation.
- *Post more than once.* Let's face it, we're all busy. There's much that slips by us. Posting several times can help ensure your message is out there. Beware, however, too much of a "good thing" can be detrimental. A constant barrage of posts or tweets can cause your followers to unfriend or unfollow you, or ignore future posts, losing you potential future support. Post something new each time. For example, first post asks for the item, the next one states how many items received (*to date we've only received a few or half of what we need*), and subsequent posts continue to follow up on progress or completion (*we're almost at our target goal, just a few more. Please help!*). This way you're posting about the project several times, but it's not same message. Finally, what should your posts say other than asking for resources? Say thanks to the community for their support and show appreciation and recognition for your youth volunteers. Share what you're doing and why you're doing it so that when you ask for donations you'll get a better response.
- *A picture is worth a thousand words.* Include lots of pictures in your posts. Visuals help human-ize your project and engage your audience. When working with youth under 18 years of age, parental permission is usually required when posting online or publishing. Your school, library, or organization may already have a photo waiver or policy in place. Check this out prior to com-mencement and implementation. When in doubt, pictures of finished products or empty supply boxes waiting to be filled are good choices. Images of youth at work can still be added. Just shoot images from behind or from up above capturing the back of the child's head or his or her hands in action.

In addition to sharing what you're doing, invite board members to your activities. Show stakeholders what you're accomplishing. When stakeholders know what you're doing, there will be more buy-in and support provided.

How Much Do I Need?

Funding for a maker service project will vary greatly. Many of the projects listed can be accomplishment with little to no cost. Review the projects prior to commencement to see which will be a good match for your youth and your budget. Estimate the costs of the project from the noted supply list. Be sure to include not only the listed items but also items and services such as photocopying and postage. Work with local groups to cut down on shipping costs and transportations costs. Often there are coworkers or community members who can pitch in and help deliver items. While it is nice for youth to deliver the items they have made, it can sometimes be cost prohibitive to provide transportation. Invite community partners to your library for pickup and a photo op, if schedules permit. Network with other librarians in your area with similar programs and share resources. Your surplus causing storage issues can be put to good use. Gestures of goodwill help all librarians support their programming endeavors.

4

Partnerships, Collaboration, and Communication

Alone we can do so little; together we can do so much.
—Helen Keller

Strong partnerships and effective communication need to be developed and nurtured, as they are the key to a successful program. This chapter addresses cultivating partnerships and working with outside agencies and nonprofits, as well as collaborating with staff within the school. Sometimes we see the word *collaboration* with a negative connotation based on prior bad experiences. The key is to make collaboration a positive experience for all parties involved, including yourself! It's about developing relationships and respect, and it's a process that won't happen overnight but will be worth the eventual outcome. Remember, it's not about the projects, it's about partnerships. One needs only to review comments on social media groups to discover this important caveat: post after post decrying sadness and frustration that a donation was not accepted. After all the time and energy invested, you want your donation accepted and put to good use. Just because a service project is in this book or on a blog or social media site, it doesn't mean your local agency needs, wants, or will accept the donation, particularly when donations involve medical facilities, ill recipients, or live animals. Every community and facility is unique. The key is in planning and communication, critical steps in successful collaborations.

SUCCESSFUL COLLABORATION

Our MakerCare service program at Islip High School is successful not just because our students perform needed services for the community. We provide numerous opportunities for our students and community partners due to positive, effective collaboration. What is the recipe for successful collaborations? Follow these easy recommendations:

- Keep it simple.
- Respect time.
- Be flexible.
- Say thank you.

Keep it simple. Start with small projects, then work your way up to more complex projects. With successful collaboration, organizations will want to continue the relationship and may even begin to initiate future collaborative projects. The memory of a negative experience lasts a long time and leads to a feeling of wasted time, energy, and effort.

Respect time. Time is the one thing we cannot replace. Once it's gone, we can no longer recover it. Be respectful of the time commitments others make, as they should be of yours. Mutual respect for time builds strong relationships and leads to less frustration.

Be flexible. Be receptive to the needs of the organization. There are times where you may have one project in mind only to be told the organization is saturated with that item. Open dialogue and be proactive to the needs of the organization. This makes more sense—to help those in need, in the way needed the most. Don't waste time and money buying supplies and organizing volunteers on a project only to discover your contribution is either not needed at this time or could have been completed under different guidelines making the final product more desirable. Before engaging youth groups to make dog toys for your local animal shelter, stop by the shelter with samples in hand. Meet with the director or a vet tech and be sure to introduce yourself to the reception staff. The receptionists are the ones who help get you in touch with those you need, answer your questions over the phone, and it's nice to put a name with a face. They are most likely the ones to receive your donation when dropping off. The conversation will start off with the obligatory, "thank you so much" but will turn into a more detailed and productive conversation when you query, "Are these what you want?" "Do you have a preference?" "How could we make this better?" "What else can you use?" The agency's representatives will realize you are receptive to constructive criticism and will let loose with very specific requirements. I've had representatives go into the back storeroom to obtain samples of finished products they didn't want, as these items are harmful to the animals. Imagine that! Some service clubs thought they were doing a good job and helping animals in need, yet their contribution was potentially harmful and not what was needed or wanted. Those donations were still accepted and the photo op taken as these organizations are on a shoestring budget and can't afford to turn away help or turn off potential donors. Shelters often receive cat toy donations with an overhand stitch that poses a risk to cats as their claws can get stuck in the stitching. An inseam made by sewing machines is preferable. If you have a sewing teacher or sewing club, collaborate to provide safe toys for shelter cats. This initial layer of communication produces mutually beneficial results as both parties walk away satisfied. Sewing students learn a basic stitch on sewing machines giving them experience needed for their curriculum, while producing an authentic item desperately needed in the community. Remember the best laid plans often go awry; be flexible!

Say thank you. The most important part of maintaining a collaborative partnership is the simple act of saying "thank you." Both the organization and your group should share experiences with each other: a quick thank you for a successful partnership, or note expressing the sentiment of your group, what they experienced, and how they felt to be part of the endeavor. Pictures sent through e-mail or, better still, shared on social media highlighting the group's effort bring attention to the organization and your program. Mutual gratitude goes a long way in establishing strong, solid relationships that continue year after year. Let's face it, we all want to work with nice people who value our time, energy, and effort. Who wouldn't?

PARTNERSHIPS

Librarians are natural connectors. We make a habit of connecting people to needs, so why not connect groups? We are community builders and we share a lot. What better combination! When making and developing contacts, start within your own organization. There are many connections to be made through colleagues who "know" people. Do not overlook the benefits of networking with associates and acquaintances of your colleagues, friends, and neighbors, as this broadens your contact list of groups with whom you can collaborate.

Your community partners can be any one of the following: government agencies, social service organizations, businesses, and educational institutions. There are many local, national, and global organizations available, as well. Partners bring together needs and skills, and every partnership is unique.

Youth

Most teens volunteer to help others and not because it "looks good on a resume" (Parker & Franco 1999, 171; Corporation for National & Community Service Issue Brief 2005). Some young people recognize the benefits of volunteering and how this reflects on resumes and college applications and therefore seek out opportunities to bolster these documents. Keep in mind though "the majority of volunteer work done by young people is not done because of mandates, but personal motivation" and "63% of young volunteers have no requirements" (DoSomething.org 2012, 20). Youth want to volunteer with a friend and find the social experience desirable (Parker & Franco 1999, 171; DoSomething.org 2007, 29). According to Parker and Franco, "36 percent would participate in service if a friend asked, and about 26 percent would if they could do it in a group" (1999, 171). When working with youth, plan group programs, particularly Bring-a-Friend events. When advertising programs to youth, statistically high school students are more likely to volunteer and volunteer regularly than junior high school students (Grimm, Dietz, Spring, Arey, & Foster-Bey 2005). Customize your programming to address the characteristics of youth volunteers as discussed in Chapter 1.

Schools

Many schools already have service-based clubs, such as National Honor Society, Key Club, Red Cross Club, Interact, and Habitat for Humanity. Cultivate a partnership with groups that already exist and already have a service agenda as club advisors are always looking for service opportunities. This scenario is simplest for all. If you're a school librarian, begin by inviting service clubs in your school to hold a meeting in your library or makerspace. Service clubs typically need to carry out hands-on service projects that benefit the school or community at large and consequently are always looking for new ways to contribute. You'll be collaborating weekly with students and advisors. Once you're comfortable with this format, invite other school groups to join in. The art club, maker club, and craft club are sound choices to include for the obvious reasons. According to a DoSomething.org survey, "Young people who work out on a sports team are 18% more likely to have volunteered than those who work out on their own" (DoSomething.org 2012, 10). With this in mind, some collaboration with your school sports teams may warrant an investigation.

Other school personnel you should consider collaborating with are your Family and Consumer Science (FACS) staff and art teachers. These educators can provide assistance with craft-based activities. From advice to an extra pair of hands, they are go-to people in schools. Sewing classes need projects that will help them learn stitches, both by hand and by machine. A collaborative partnership enhances the curriculum while providing needed community service. Youth learn through authentic projects in this advantageous partnership.

Community-Based Service Clubs

Community-based service clubs such as 4-H, Scouts, YMCA, CYO, Boys and Girls Clubs are another potential collaborative association. Libraries can support other community-based organizations in their neighborhood. It's not productive when community agencies all vie for the same pool of youth participants. Working together allows us to get more accomplished.

Local Government and Nongovernmental Organizations

Every community consists of organizations that provide comfort and well-being to area residents. Faith-based organizations, animal shelters, health-care facilities are just a few of the government and nongovernmental organizations in your neighborhood. As donors we often gravitate to the largest, most visible establishments causing a surplus, while smaller organizations struggle. These smaller agencies need your help.

Think of alternatives within these groups. Don't overlook similar alliances. The results are the same, by getting items to those who need your group's handiwork. For example, if your local hospital has an overabundance of newborn knitted caps and can't accept donations from yet another service group, then seek out and work with a local midwife instead. As an alternative to your town animal shelter, contact local rescue groups. There's always someone in your community who needs help. Spread the giving around so all receive assistance. Set up these partnerships in advance rather than after items have been made.

National Government and Nongovernmental Organizations

Many large national organizations have local offices; start there as your efforts remain local and benefit your community while reducing your expenses on transportation and shipping costs related to your donations. Working with a local office of a national organization tailors your efforts to best benefit those within your community as local offices are more familiar with the needs in your area. Just because you see a great idea for a project on the organization's official website, it doesn't mean there's a specific need for that item in your area. I remember calling a local Habitat for Humanity office and suggesting we make Welcome Home signs, and discovered they were not really needed. It seems the signs are one of the most visible projects and everyone from scouts to schools creates and donates these items. I suggested key ring holders, and my Habitat volunteer coordinator had never had this as a donation, even though it is listed as one of the activities on Habitat's national website. The point is, don't make any assumptions, communicate. Open up a dialogue and discover how you can initiate a mutually positive experience: one where everyone benefits from the experience and time and funds are not wasted.

Global Outreach

There are many global causes that need support. Working with groups providing assistance overseas adds additional considerations to your collaborations, notably the cost of shipping items overseas or to the organization's central office. Often these groups need funds for shipping and other expenditures. If you want to help one of these groups but the costs seem prohibitive, consider organizing a craft sale fund-raiser and donate the proceeds to the organization of your choice or use the funds to implement and ship the project.

Individuals

Once your program is off the ground and your group is established, reach out to individuals in your community, though more likely the opposite will occur. Through your outreach and social media efforts, community members will seek you out for a potential partnership. The Cerebral Palsy Bib project originated from just such a request. The nephew of a colleague, diagnosed with cerebral palsy, needed absorbent cloth bibs due to over salivation, a side effect of his medical condition. The child's mother had used a vendor for this, but when they ceased producing the item, it left the family with limited options. This is an excellent example of helping individual members of your community. Using a sample bib, our sewing teacher deconstructed it to develop a suitable template. The bibs use a simple straight stitch, and this project was offered to our students who finished their other sewing work early: a beautiful way to keep students engaged and aid a staff member. This book showcases examples such as these as it may spark ideas for working within your community. A project may start out to benefit an individual but then grow to aid a local agency or vice versa. Whether aiding a colleague, your local United Cerebral Palsy facility, or support group in your area, the bibs are needed in each scenario. Be open and receptive, as unique opportunities present themselves.

COMMUNICATION

The single biggest problem in communication is the illusion that it has taken place.
—George Bernard Shaw

Face to Face and Phone Calls

There are many ways to communicate, and each has benefits and drawbacks. Typically, face-to-face conversations yield greater results. This is not always possible but should be attempted as the first line of collaboration when feasible. While it is better to collaborate locally, this might not always be possible and you'll need to talk to someone 400 miles away. The next best thing to a face-to-face conversation is a phone call, hearing someone's friendly voice and vice versa. The phone conversation allows for a quick change of plan and deeper collaboration. While speaking with coordinators of volunteers, you can judge their tone of voice and hear hesitations. Be responsive and allow the coordinator to discuss their specific current needs. Yes, they'll accept what you offer, even if they don't have a need for it at that time. Here is an example of attempting to "do good" but not truly being "helpful." Being receptive to change and open to collaboration helps fulfill the organization's needs. If you listen to the description of the organization's needs and how it works to provide services, you can propose a mutually satisfactory project. By listening, communicating, and most of all, having respect for coordinator's time and the organization's need, you'll ensure a successful partnership. While your focus is to provide your teens with service projects, the organization has its specific addenda as well. Whether meeting face to face, making phone calls, or e-mailing, always remember to provide enough details and be receptive and flexible to new ideas, but most of all, get to the point. Don't waste their time or yours! Your mutual needs might not gel. If so, keep it friendly and move on. However, listen to them talk, as they may need something you can provide that you hadn't thought to offer. Many successful service projects start out this way. Remember the idea is to be helpful, not to saturate the organization that now needs to find a way to store your donations for a future use. Organizations don't like to turn away donations, as they don't want to alienate your group from helping out in the future. It's a careful balance for them, one that can be avoided with clear, open dialogue.

E-mail

My principal receives hundreds of e-mails, many of them soliciting business and some attention for their group. One such group was Postcard Pick Me Up based in Vermont. The e-mail was forwarded knowing this was "right up my alley." If unfamiliar with a group, look them up online. Always check out an organization online, either its website or social media accounts, or both, to get a feel for what they do and how they do it. This gives you a basis for engaging in further conversations with their coordinator and saves time asking questions that already have an answer online. Go the extra step and connect with group organizers. You're looking for a good fit for your youth group. Working a lot with English language learners, we thought this would be a great authentic writing exercise for our students in addition to community service. However, some of our newer entrants had limited English language proficiency, and it would be best if they wrote in their native language. E-mailing the coordinator of the organization and making inquiries confirmed the acceptance of non-English written postcards. However, at that time, cards written in Spanish were plentiful. Well, that worked out for our Turkish- and Urdu-speaking students. Communication and collaboration all wrapped up in one e-mail. Remember, you'll get more leads for new projects when others are aware of your program.

Social Media

It's been said direct messaging (DM) is the new e-mail. Many of the anecdotes in this book originated as a DM. If you're on social media such as Facebook or Twitter, this is another communication option and a great way of finding organizations to work with and connecting with other youth group leaders. Choose from numerous opportunities posted to special interest groups, then check out the organization's website, and contact information for follow-up.

Promoting Your Program

Many public libraries provide a display case for community members to highlight their hobbies, activities, and the like. Use this feature to showcase your program's work. You will generate interest in your program and gain new community supporters. You may also gain new partnerships with community organizations you didn't realize existed in your neighborhood. By consistently promoting the work your youth are engaged in you'll find donations will follow. I'm constantly stopped in the community and school hallway and asked, "what do you need?" and "what can I drop off?" Expect to be approached by those who need your help, as well. You'll need supplies to implement your projects. Some items you may have on hand, and others you'll have to purchase or solicit. When soliciting donations be sure to include what you need, why you need it, and where to drop off the requested items. Always provide contact information for those who have questions. When contacted, other items can be solicited, typically obtaining more than originally requested. Share your request through appropriate targeted listservs and e-mails. Social media is another useful communication tool. Sometimes you'll get donations, and at other times you get great leads or new partnerships, but the key is to get your message out among community stakeholders and build awareness for your program. Remember: Share your story!

Radio and TV Spots

Create a PSA, public service announcement. Radio stations have free air time set aside for public announcements. Create a 10-, 20-, or 30-second announcements. Use your makerspace's green screen, library's bookshelves as backdrop or recording studio if one is available. Schools often have a recording studio, and students who take broadcasting classes may be willing to provide their time and experience to your cause. Contact the station to inquire about specific requirements. Having contacts at local radio stations can prove beneficial not just for a short PSA, but you may find yourself on a weekly talk show! One of our supporters put me in contact with the host of a local radio show that highlights good things happening in local schools. This provides a mutual benefit. The show filled its weekly spot, and we got free advertising for our program. Local TV stations have free air time as well. Contact the station to see what special requirements are necessary and if they can provide or assist with filming. This forum typically requires professional quality work, not a teen's mobile phone video.

How to Communicate

In Appendix A, you will find several templates for calling organizations, requesting donations, and sending thank-you notes. Use these examples to establish partnerships and enrich your program. Whether calling or e-mailing an organization, be sure to be friendly, brief, and clear.

Listservs/E-mail/Social Media Post

Get your needed supplies through donations by spreading the word through local list-servs, your organization's e-mail system, or social media. Listservs are specific groups you can communicate with by subscribing to an e-mail list. Don't bombard these outlets excessively. However, judicious use of these communication platforms will inform individuals of your service group's activities and needs. Sample letters and talking points can be found in Appendix A.

Thank-You Letter

It's understandable to expect a thank-you from the organization you supplied with donations. However, for a successful partnership sharing what you learned and how you felt about the partnership can reap benefits. People want to work with nice people and who recognize their efforts, and this applies to both the donor and the receiver. It is beneficial for you and your teens to go the step further to seal and cement a positive partnership with a quick note of thanks. Staff members of charitable organizations work exceptionally hard with limited recognition. Own up to any faults or difficulties experienced, but this is not a venue for complaints.

The "F" Word: Failure

Yes, failure *is* an option and it occurs more frequently than we'd like. As discussed in an earlier chapter, failure can lead to success, and in this case successful partnerships. Each interaction with a service organization and each project is unique and subject to unforeseen problems. Every experience, positive or negative, is a learning experience. We learn from doing, and each failure provides us with life experience. Truman Capote described failure as "the condiment that gives success its flavor." Addressing issues by analyzing the situation helps prevent recurrence. Reflect on how to handle a partnership better and apply to future scenarios.

When my group first started out making plastic yarn (plarn) from plastic grocery bags we thought, "this isn't difficult." And truthfully it isn't. It is, however, quite time consuming and labor intensive. Had we needed to complete the intended item by a certain time, it would have been with great difficulty. With several projects we also discovered some pitfalls and concerns, so the projects section includes a caveats segment for you to learn from the failures of others. Keep in mind, even with meticulous planning, things can go awry. Learn from the situation and move forward.

In the world of nonprofits, changes in staffing occur frequently and can lead to a change in the community partnership even midway through a project. The ability to adapt and overcome is a critical trait and not just for Marines! We all benefit from this mantra. When an unsuccessful situation arises, be sure to analyze and reflect why the situation occurred. Blaming or pointing fingers is not productive. Model civility, constructive planning, and decision making because youth have limited experience in these areas. This positive educational experience will serve youth throughout their lives and careers. Critical reflection is beneficial for future situations; critical blame is not. Valuable lessons such as conflict resolution, grit, and flexibility are advantageous for life beyond youth service participation.

Part II

INTRODUCTION TO SERVICE PROJECTS

I have been impressed with the urgency of doing.
Knowing is not enough; we must apply.
Being willing is not enough; we must do.
—Leonardo da Vinci

When striving to make a difference, choose attainable goals. We all wish for world peace. However, selecting realistic projects with reachable goals ensures youth have a positive experience and a positive influence on their communities. The second section of this book features numerous hands-on service projects young people can make. Start your maker journey by choosing a problem your youth care about. Youth reported they were "more likely to participate if they knew someone who benefitted" (Parker & Franco 1999, 171). When picking projects, young people typically want to help others, so humanize the project (DoSomething.org 2007, 29). Picking up trash along the side of the road helps the environment and is undoubtedly a worthy endeavor. But teens like a human connection when volunteering, and you might find greater participation if your group collects plastic bags to upcycle for a project. These bags are routinely thrown out and end up in garbage dumps where it will take over 20 years to decompose. Using 500–700 plastic bags, your group can help the environment and make sleep mats for the homeless or using 20–30 bags to make jump ropes for afterschool programs. We want to save the world, but there's a part of us that needs reassurance that we are making a difference in changing a life or situation.

Some readers may have started reading this section first eager to get started making a difference. However, it's not just the projects but the partnerships that determine your success. There are many nationally known organizations and no doubt numerous agencies in your community. The more familiar you are with the activities of local nonprofits in your area, the more opportunities are available for youth. Try to follow as many of these groups as you can on social media. One of our local nonprofits needed holiday decorations for its Breakfast with Santa fund-raiser. On its Facebook group page, the organization put a call out for help to service groups looking for participants to donate handmade decorations to brighten its festivities. Not all maker service projects will be found in the following pages. As noted earlier, some activities are a onetime need fulfilled and often publicized on social media or through networking. The importance of interaction and communication between your youth group and nonprofits in your area cannot be stressed enough.

In this section, there is a mix of different types of projects from arts-based to sewing and yarn crafts, as well as technology-based projects. Keep in mind, you can mix tech and nontech projects. Your group can crochet scarves or blankets for hospitals and shelters, but what to do if you don't have enough crochet hooks? That's OK, go to your favorite open source design community, such as Thingiverse, and just 3D print as many crochet hooks as you need!

Programs should be as inclusive as possible. Have left-handed scissors available and provide instructions for both right- and left-handed crocheting. Often a right-handed youth advisor will have a hard time demonstrating proper techniques. Find clear instructions and images online from the Crochet Guild of America (www.crochet.org/?page=stitches-lefthand) or purchase a copy of *I Can't Believe I'm Crocheting!* (2006) for clear step-by-step right- and left-handed instructions. There's nothing sadder than an unsuccessful young participant looking to you for guidance.

Many of the projects will list resources and directions available in languages other than English. If your community has a large population of non–English proficient youths, look for these projects. Obtain these resources prior to program commencement.

Encourage youth to initiate projects and choose charities to support. Allow youth a voice to identify authentic concerns and develop the goals needed to implement positive changes in their community. Be sure to obtain necessary permissions needed to implement your project. It may be a principal, buildings' supervisor, or town official. This is noted in the project descriptions in the following chapters. Also, when planning to implement a project, determine if it is ongoing or a onetime commitment, where the funding will come from and which group of youths is better suited to carrying out the project.

MAKER FUND-RAISERS—SHOW ME THE MONEY!

Does your youth group need to raise funds to pay for supplies, for shipping donations, or simply to donate to a chosen cause? Overseas organizations need funds and a financial contribution is the best course of action. In these cases, below are a few suggestions supporting youth makers in their quest to raise necessary funds through maker activities.

One of our special education students decided she wanted to raise money to help local families battling cancer. She produced handmade necklaces, bracelets, and keychains using unique beads. Her table was set up in the faculty room for a two-week period. She created a colorful informative flyer marketing her event, arranged her wares on her given table, and in all was successful in helping the community. Obviously, more crafters, more funds can be raised. So host a craft fair!

Project: Craft Fair
Description: Using many of the ideas found in this book as well as additional do-it-yourself (DIY) craft ideas, make a variety of saleable items using low to no cost supplies. Proceeds benefit the organization of your group's choosing. This is a great way to get your teens researching organizations and causes. Some teens will approach you with an organization in mind due to a family member or close acquaintance who is affected by the situation or illness. The craft fair need not be a stand-alone, but can piggyback on an existing event such as a town holiday fair or at a spring concert or other community event, such as a community annual yard sale. There are many groups raising money for charity through selling handcrafted items online. An online store crafting for charity provides a long-standing project for a school group, possibly one partnered with a business or marketing class.

Project: Host a Philanthro-Party
Description: Everyone loves a party, so invite your community to *a party with a purpose!* Raise funds and awareness while having fun. All you need to do is pick a cause and plan your party. Funds raised benefit the cause chosen. Some theme-based inspirational ideas can be found in the book *Philanthroparties* (Cerone 2017).

Project: E4K—Endure for Kindness
Description: E4K is a program sponsored by Random Acts of Kindness organization during the month of April. This endurance event stresses 24 hours of doing a kind act, or however long you can hold out! Have your group organize a community-wide event.

Project: Art Book
Description: Students at Bernards High School, New Jersey, designed and illustrated a coloring book, *Color for a Cause* (2016), to benefit cancer patients. Some teens drew the

images, and others scanned the sheets into digital images for book production. Proceeds benefit cancer patients, and for every book sold, one is donated to local cancer treatment centers. Books are sold online through Amazon. This is a creative option for artistic youth groups.

Project: Art Show
Description: Using your makerspace supplies have youth create artwork to be displayed and sold. Paintings, sculptures, and mixed media are a few options. Host a showing or a sale. The proceeds go to the organization of your group's choosing. This will require planning and an event location if not using your library.

Project: Trash to Fashion Show
Description: Host this event with one group, such as one school or district, or open it up to several towns or countywide. It's up to you how large you want the event to be. Keep in mind it's best to start small, but you'll need enough participation so a larger population pool might be necessary. Youth create outfits made from recycled books, melted beach balls, or snack bags! The event highlights design and creativity through upcycling everyday items. Charge admission to the show and sell raffles and handmade items to raise funds for a cause chosen by your group. Think of all the skills your group will need: planning, time management, marketing, and of course design, creativity, sewing, and making. A few things to keep in mind, this requires a lot of planning and marketing or your event won't be successful. Draw up guidelines and rules of participation before you advertise the event. What materials can't be used, for example, fabric; guidelines such as you want the kids to wear clothing under their creations in case of wardrobe malfunctions; and critical dates are a few items to consider. Have youth participate in teams of three to four members: a model and one or two designer-creators. Teams probably shouldn't have more than four members for manageability and you should encourage them to come up with a team name. One of our teams was called Juicy Couture as the dress and matching handbag was made of juice pouches! Find a volunteer emcee for the event, someone lively and chatty. If you're not hosting this event at your library or school, find a suitable location. To advertise the event, send flyers and notifications to local school e-mails and listservs. Social media is your ally for marketing this event. Support youth participation in your library by hosting brainstorming and making sessions in addition to planning meetings.

Project: Setting Up a Crowd Source Fund-Raiser
Description: Using a platform such as GoFundMe, help youth take the initiative to fund a cause. Youth learn how to digitally fund-raise. There's potential job experience for a budding NGO employee. Use of multiple organizational skills, planning, coordinating, communicating, and of course leadership are used.

What do all these projects have in common? Communication, organization, teamwork, planning, and marketing. Real-world skills and potential career options are particularly useful for those seeking employment with nonprofits and corporate offices alike. These projects require youth not only creating and making, but also taking a leadership role. Librarians can empower youth to bring about positive change.

5

Animal Welfare

No act of kindness, no matter how small, is ever wasted.
—Aesop

Children often relate to animals. An easy way to foster compassionate behavior in your students is by contacting your local animal shelter and inquiring what types of donations are needed. Many local animal shelters will accept bedding, toys, and homemade treats. There are numerous online tutorials for creating all of these items. Choose either a no-sew or sewing-required bedding pattern depending on age range and skill of your youth participants. Dogs are often bored being kenneled all day, and joy can be brought to them by creating a simple toy made by using a tennis ball and upcycled fabric rope. Not all shelters will accept homemade treats, but if yours does, there are simple recipes to create tasty treats for our furry friends. Just think of the added academic benefits for students who will have to measure, add fractions when doubling the recipe, and read and follow recipe directions. Always call your local animal shelter or rescue group in advance to ensure they will accept these types of donations; many will have special requirements. Determine this in advance and plan your activity accordingly. Communication and collaboration are the two elements most needed when working with community agencies.

According to the ASPCA, nationally there are over 6.5 million animals entering our shelters annually ("Pet Statistics"). These numbers refer only to shelters and not the countless rescue groups nationwide. With so many animals and community agencies tasked with alleviating the situation in need of assistance, this is a good place to start.

CALENDAR

Here are a few specific animal-related events and celebrations to plan your programming:

Be Kind to Animals Week (May, first week)
National Craft for Your Local Shelter Day (July 21)
National Dog Day (August 26)
Prevention to Cruelty to Animals Month (April)

Use stencils to decorate doggy bandanas. Photo credit: Elaine Schmidt

DOGS

Project: DOG BANDANA

Description: These handmade bandanas are great for pet adoption events making the dogs look stylish as they greet their prospective forever families. Or, pair the bandanas with a treat and give these items as a gift for the adoptive family particularly during an adoption fair. Be sure to choose colorful, fun fabric. You want the dogs to look their best!

Community Partners: Your town animal shelter, rescue groups in your area.

Materials Needed: Washable fabric, measuring tape or ruler, pinking shears or sewing machine, and thread.

Instructions: Fold a 20-inch fabric square diagonally and cut on the crease to make two scarves 20 × 20 × 30 inches. To prevent fraying, sew the edges with a sewing machine or, even simpler, use pinking shears to cut the edges. The no-sew option using just the pinking shears can be accomplished by elementary school children and up, provided they can use a measuring tape and scissors. Sewing a straight stitch using a sewing machine can be handled by most tweens and any willing teenager.

Project: BRAIDED DOG TOY

Description: Dogs kenneled in animal shelters are bored and need an outlet. A simple braided chew toy can brighten their day. All necessary supplies are derived from upcycled, donated materials making this project no cost.

Community Partners: Animal shelters and rescue groups.

Materials Needed: Upcycled T-shirts, scissors, and instructions on how to braid for those learning to braid for the first time.

Instructions: This is a low difficulty level service project with high impact and great results. First start off with a T-shirt drive. A mix of sizes is helpful. Adult sizes Small to XL can make many more toys than just youth sizes. Be sure to let donors know you'll accept T-shirts with stains or small tears. You'll get more fabric donated, and after you cut the strips and braid the fabric, no one will ever know there were imperfections. Lay shirt on a flat surface. Cut 2–3 inch wide strips across the width of the shirt. Size of the shirt will determine how many strips you'll have. Wider strips make thicker braids for larger dogs. Thin strips are suitable for small breeds. Using three strips, tie a knot at one end and begin braiding using instruction sheet on how to braid. This is also something that could be modeled by pairing youth together with one who knows how to braid while the other learns. Optional supplies—book or duct tape to hold down one end while braiding, if the child is not coordinated enough to hold fabric and braid simultaneously. Again, you can pair children—one holds and one braids.

Caveats: You'll need to make a variety of sizes for the range of breeds you'll find in a shelter, from tiny Yorkies to the larger German Shep-

Cut old T-shirts into strips and braid.

herds, small and thin for smaller breeds and larger, thicker toys for large breed dogs such as Rottweilers and Labs. When working with a rescue group, the toys can be homogenous based on the breed.

Since you'll be cutting a lot of fabric, having a pair of fabric scissors is advantageous. Keep an eye on these expensive cutting tools as youth may not be aware that cutting anything but fabric with a fabric scissor will ruin the blades. Be sure to explain their proper care.

Modification: Braided Dog Toy with Tennis Ball.

Materials Needed: Boxcutters, needle-nose pliers, tennis balls.

Instructions: The braids can be inserted into tennis balls making this toy more enjoyable. Tennis balls can be upcycled from a high school tennis team or a local athletic club. Both groups typically have dead tennis balls available to be upcycled. Be sure to call around

for donations. Using a boxcutter or other sharp edge, create a slit or X at both ends of the ball. Pull the braid through using needle-nose pliers or similar tool.

Caveats: Sharp tools will need to be used so the age of your participants should reflect the maturity needed to work with these items. Otherwise, you'll need to prep the tennis balls prior to the activity.

Project: DOG TREATS
Description: Yummy, healthy snacks are always a treat!
Community Partners: Animal shelters or rescue groups.
Materials Needed: Items from the recipe, spoons, forks, mixing bowls, cookie trays; cooking spray to grease the trays; access to an oven; plastic bag or container to store treats.

Recipe for Pumpkin Molasses Treats:

- ½ cup canned pumpkin
- 4 tbsp molasses
- 4 tbsp water
- 2 tbsp vegetable oil
- 2 cups whole wheat flour
- ¼ tsp baking soda   .
- ¼ tsp baking powder
- 1 tsp cinnamon (optional)

Instructions: Preheat oven to 350 degrees. Mix the wet ingredients together in a bowl: first four ingredients. Add the remaining ingredients to the mixture and stir. Scoop up a teaspoon of dough and roll into balls using your hands. Wet hands work best. Place balls onto a lightly greased cookie sheet and flatten with a fork. Bake approximately 25 minutes.

Money Saver: Canned pumpkin is usually on sale prior to and after Thanksgiving; stock up!

Caveats: Check with your donor partner and see what's permissible prior to beginning this project. Each organization will have specific needs and requirements. Some dogs have allergies or medical conditions and alternative ingredients may be necessary.

Modifications: There are many no-bake treat recipes if you don't have access to an oven. You'll have to find the right community partners to ensure they'll take these snacks.

Project: OUTDOOR DOG SHELTER

Description: Make a simple A-frame dog house!

Community Partners: Many animal rescue groups are interested in obtaining these houses. Be sure to find a partner prior to beginning this project.

Materials Needed: Instructions can be found on several reliable sites such as DIY Network and Loewe's. Find a pattern that your group can confidently complete. Your school may have a shop class available to cut wood for this project. If not, many lumber and home stores will cut wood for your group. Gather the wood and have students assemble the outdoor dog house. If working indoors, you can place a drop cloth on the floor prior to staining or painting. Art students are a great resource for adding style to your outdoor abode!

CATS

Project: EGGS-TRA SPECIAL CAT TOY

Description: Make a fun rolling toy for bored cats.

Materials Needed: Plastic eggs (the kind sold around Easter time), glue (either a craft glue—Tacky Glue or hot glue gun can be used), permanent markers in various colors, dry cat food.

Instructions: Fill a clean plastic egg with a small amount of dry cat food. Glue the egg shut and be sure to wipe off any extra glue. Allow the glue to dry and then decorate with the markers.

Caveat: Don't fill the egg with indigestible items, such as bells, as this can pose a hazard to the animals if ingested. Using plastic eggs is a nice way to upcycle the surplus of springtime plastic eggs.

Money Saver: Run a collection drive after Easter or buy discounted surplus after the holiday.

Modification: Ping Pong Cat Toy.

Materials Needed: Ping pong balls, paint or permanent markers.

If you can't find plastic eggs, ping pong balls can be decorated with nontoxic paint or permanent markers.

Assorted handmade cat toys.

Project: CAT JINGLE BALL TOY

Description: Delightful ball made of melted hot glue; includes a bell or two inside the two halves prior to completion. The ball rolls in unexpected ways due to the unevenness of the dried glue making the toy highly engaging.

Age Range/Difficulty: This project requires patience and the use of hot glue. Recommended for grades 6–12.

Community Partners: Animal shelters and rescue groups.

Materials Needed: Hot glue gun, glue sticks, white glue and a brush for application, small rubber ball—one that you can squeeze, jingle bell, nail polish.

Instructions: Mount the rubber ball on the top of the handle nail polish bottle using a dot of hot glue. Cover the top half of the rubber ball with white glue and allow to dry. Then, cover the top half of the ball with hot glue using a crisscross pattern or individual dots. Pause and allow glue to dry and harden between applications. This cannot be done in one step. You need to wait for glue to dry before covering more of the surface. Be sure all space is covered with glue and allow time to dry completely. Squeeze the bottom of the rubber ball to pop off the dried, hardened glue half. Repeat steps above so that you have two halves. Insert 1–2 jingle bells. Buy these in the dollar store around the holiday season. Hot glue the two halves together. Allow time to dry. The ball can be a bit lopsided. The beauty is that the ball will roll in unexpected ways, further engaging the feline. Optional: Use your choice of color nail polish to coat the ball or leave natural.

Caveat: Depending on the size of your group, you will need quite a few electrical outlets and glue guns.

Project: FABRIC CATNIP SQUARES

Community Partners: Animal shelters and rescue groups. Partner with the Family and Consumer Science teachers at your local school or in your building. This project is a great way to learn a straight stitch. Many public libraries have sewing groups, too.

Materials Needed: Fabric, Poly-Fil, catnip, needles and thread, sewing machine.

Instructions: Make squares of fabric approximately 2–4 inches. Sew the sides together with the insides facing each other leaving one side open. Right the fabric turning it inside

out. Insert fiber filling and a dash of catnip. Then sew up the remaining side.

Caveats: If finishing off with a hand stitch, you need to make sure the stitches are extremely tight and close. Any loose thread can catch a cat's claw and could cause potential harm to the animal. Some shelters will accept these items, but you will have to assign a staff member or volunteer to supervise play.

Project: UPCYCLED CATNIP SOCK TOYS
Description: Make cat toys from a variety of upcycled items.
Materials Needed: Upcycled children's socks or toddler mittens, Poly-Fil, catnip, Mylar (upcycled from deflated balloons or wine bottle gift bags), jingle bells, small hair bands. Optional: Needle and thread.
Instructions: Depending on sock size. See below.

> *Infant/toddler sock or mitten:* Stuff sock with Poly-Fil stuffing and half a teaspoon of catnip or stuff with Mylar and catnip. Bell optional. Sew the top of the sock with very small, tight (invisible) stitches using a needle and thread or use sewing machine if available.

Caveat: Stitches need to be exceptionally small and tight as visible stitches can injure a cat's claw if caught. This is a teachable moment for youth. Our service is to help, not cause harm. Some shelters will not accept an overhand stitch, so be sure to have a discussion with your community partner to ensure items are donatable.

> *Child/adult long knee-high sock:* You will divide the sock into sections when filling it. In the toe section, fill with Poly-Fil stuffing and half a teaspoon of catnip. Tie off that section with a fabric hair band that can be purchased at the local dollar store. In the next section, the heel, fill with Poly-Fil and 2–3 bells, also found at the dollar store. Tie off with a hair band. In the next section stuff with Mylar, tie off, and finally in the last section add some Poly-Fil and half a teaspoon of catnip. Tie a knot in the end of the sock to seal. You may sew the end shut, but tying a knot is secure enough and makes this a no-sew project accessible for most ages and abilities.

Caveats: Mylar is not digestible. Consumption can cause severe gastric distress in small animals. Check with your community partners to see if they will accept Mylar-filled toys. If the animals are supervised during play, this should not pose a problem. Be sure to ask. The Mylar can be omitted; substitute with Poly-Fil stuffing instead.
Tip: Celebrate Lost Sock Memorial Day (May 9); a great way to upcycle those lone socks!

Project: FLUFFY FLEECE CAT TOY

Description: Make a fluffy pom-pom-style cat toy.

Community Partners: Animal shelters and rescue groups.

Materials Needed: Fleece cut into strips ½ to 1 inch wide, cardboard cut to 3 × 6 inches, scissors. Most fleece sold is 58–60 inches long or you can use fleece scraps for this project.

Instructions: Wrap the fleece strips around the 3-inch part of the cardboard, careful not to pull too tight. You'll need three to six strips of fleece, depending on how full and fluffy you want this toy. When finished wrapping the first strip, place the second strip near or next to the first one and continue wrapping. Repeat for remaining strips until you have covered the cardboard

with only one inch showing on either side. Next, slide the fleece off the cardboard. Using a 1 × 6-inch piece of fleece, slide under the wrapped pieces and tie a knot in the middle. With your scissor, cut the ends of the loops on both sides. Trim fleece, if desired. Fluff up the fleece.

Modification: If you only have small scraps on hand, do not worry. It's always better to upcycle donated supplies than purchasing new material. Cut the fleece into ½ × 4-inch strips. Line up the strips on top of each other. Use approximately 20. Remember more strips, the fluffier. Next, using heavy-duty string, tie a knot around the center of the fleece strips. Wrap string around a few times tying knots as you go. Cut off any excess string. Fluff the fleece up by peeling the strips back.

PET ITEMS

Project: UPCYCLED OLD SWEATER PET BEDDING

Description: Make a comfy pet bed!

Community Partners: Rescue groups

Materials Needed: Upcycled old sweater, Poly-Fil, needle, and thread.

Instructions: Stich collar closed. Stich across the sweater from under armpit to the other armpit. Stuff the sleeves with Poly-Fil. Insert a standard size throw pillow or Poly-Fil in the body portion of the sweater. Sew the bottom of the sweater closed. Now attach the sleeves to the body of the main sweater, sewing it together to form a ring for the bedding.

Caveat: This project requires quite a bit of sewing to complete. Youth need to make tight, neat stitches.

Project: NO-SEW PET BEDDING

Description: Easy-to-make bedding for cats or dogs.

Materials Needed: For one bed, you'll need two 30 × 36-inch pieces of fleece, approximately 48-oz polyester fiberfill (Poly-Fil), and scissors.

Instructions: Lay fleece right-side together. Cut 5-inch square from each corner of the fleece. Cut fringe edges 5 inches into fleece at l-inch intervals around top and bottom layers. Knot fringes together around three sides of blanket. Insert the Poly-Fil stuffing (or a pillow form) into bed. Knot remaining sides of bed.

Project: HEATING PADS FOR POST-SURGICAL ANIMALS

Description: Rice-filled packs for animals provide comfort following surgery.

Community Partners: Animal hospitals, veterinarians, and shelters.

Materials Needed: Fabric, sewing machine or needle, thread, rice.

Instructions: Cotton fabric or upcycled sheets, pillowcases, or flannel can be used. Cut fabric 12 × 6 inches and fold in half with the right sides facing each other. Sew the long sides and one end. Unfold the fabric to make the fabric right-side out. Fill approximately ⅔ full with rice and stich the end closed.

Caveat: Line up a community partner prior to initiating any project, particularly health-related projects. Not all health-care facilities will accept your donations. Query first.

BIRDS

Project: BIRDSEED ORNAMENTS
Description: Birds get hungry, particularly in the winter. This is a good way you can promote participation in community bird counts and help out hungry birds.

Community Partner: Your own campus and patrons! Feed your local bird population. A high school ornithology class. A great way to learn and do! Local Audubon group.

Materials Needed: Birdseed, gelatin, water, flour, straws, twine, wax paper, measuring cups, bowls for mixing, spoons for stirring. To mold the ornaments, you can use cookie cutters or use the metal lids from canning jars (Mason). They're the perfect shape and size, and it's inexpensive enough to purchase an adequate supply for a group project. As an option, the lids/molds can be upcycled from the community.

Instructions:

Recipe:

- ¾ cup flour
- ½ cup water
- 1 packet unflavored gelatin
- 3 tbsp corn syrup
- 4 cups birdseed

1. Mix flour, water, and gelatin together in a large bowl.
2. Add the birdseed to the mixture. Stir until mixed.
3. Spray molds with cooking spray. Add the birdseed mixture to the molds pressing down fingers or bottom of measuring cup to pack the mold.
4. Poke a hole at the top of the mold using the straw. You can cut the straws into thirds to save on supplies. Be sure the straw goes through completely as you'll need to get an 8- to 10-inch length of string through the hole after the ornament has completely dried. Tie a knot in the string once you've passed it through the hole.
5. Leave the birdseed to dry for 2–3 hours. Then remove the ornaments placing them on wax paper so the other side may dry.
6. When ornaments are completely dry, place string or twine through the hole so that they may be hung on a tree.

When birds are finished eating the seeds, they may recycle the string to line their nests. **Caveat:** Be aware of nut allergies.

Project: BIRD STRIKE DETERRENT
Description: Does your school or library have large glass windows? Have you experienced birds striking the glass only to find their lifeless bodies on the front lawn? Birds do not see glass. They see the reflection of their habitat and continue to fly until it's too late. According to the Cornell Lab of Ornithology, "Up to 100 million birds are killed each year by collisions with windows" (2016). In this project, you will be protecting wildlife and upcycling old technology. With streaming services and cloud storage available, CDs are being used less and less. Upcycle those discs!
Community Partner: Your own campus and patrons!
Materials Needed: CDs, string, ribbon, or fishing line (whatever you have available). If you want to drill a hole in the CD, you'll need a drill and bit.
Instructions: The string may go through the hole in the CD or if you have a drill in your maker area, drill a hole near the top edge of the CD and string your ribbon through the hole. You can link more than one CD to create a mobile. Hang your CD deterrents around your building and offer these items to those who need them. String can be taped to the window or if your dollar store sells suction cup hooks, use them.
Caveats: If you find an injured bird, seek professional assistance from a vet or local wildlife rehabilitator; it is not legal to keep or care for wildlife. Always contact your local animal shelter, wildlife rehabilitation group, or veterinarian for guidance when finding an injured animal.

SMALL ANIMALS

Project: RESCUE NESTS FOR BIRDS AND OTHER SMALL WILDLIFE
Description: Wildlife Rescue Nests (https://wildliferescuenests.weebly.com/) provide wildlife rehabilitators from around the world with handmade knitted nests. It has over 800 registered volunteers—both wildlife rehabilitators and knitting volunteers register on the website. Free instructions can be found on its website.
Nests are typically used for birds or small mammals. "Wildlife rehabilitators struggle to keep wild animals stress free while they are confined during the healing process . . . the nests help provide comfort to animals, reduce their stress and increase their chances of being released back into the wild" (Akande 2016).
Community Partners: Wildlife Rescue Nests. Wildlife Rescue Nests works with over 350 wildlife rehabilitation centers in the United States, Canada, and several overseas countries as well. Work with local wildlife rehabilitators in your area if you know of any. Do a quick Google search or ask local veterinarians for recommendations. Local knitters or crochet groups.
Materials Needed: Yarn (can be leftover scraps), knitting needles, free patterns from Wildlife Rescue Nest website for registered volunteers.
Instructions: Register with Wildlife Rescue Nests and access its free volunteer resources including videos and instructions. There are six types of nests that can be made in varying sizes: regular nests, which according to its website, are the most commonly requested and easiest to make. There are directions for cage-mounted regular nests also known as

"hanging nests," round cave nests, oval cave nests, hanging cave nests, and drawstring pouches. Youth can learn about the role of rehabilitation, animal survival, and release programs.

Caveat: This project should only be attempted by skilled knitters and crocheters as tension, an acquired skillset, is key to making these nests. Do not use fuzzy yarn as the animals' claws or toes can get caught in the nest causing pain and potential injury. Nests must be made with a lot of tension so that they are ridged. Floppy nests are unusable. Wildlife Rescue Nests has a strict set of policies to ensure wildlife rehabilitators receive quality nests. Attempt this project only if your youth group is sufficiently skilled. Also, do not attempt to "rescue" an animal with your group. Native wildlife is protected by federal law and can only be cared for by a licensed wildlife rehabilitator. It is unlawful to possess the animal. Always contact your local animal shelter, wildlife rehabilitation group, or veterinarian for guidance when finding an injured animal.

3D PRINTING FOR ANIMALS

The onset of 3D printing has had a positive effect on injured animals. 3D printed carts for mobility and other assistive devices for injured animals show us compassionate real-world problem solving. Bird bills are now replaced with 3D models, and custom prosthetics are becoming commonplace. Each animal embodies unique situations, and each case is handled individually. You'll need to work with local veterinarians to participate or work with a group like the CAP Program.

Project: 3D PRINTED PROSTHETICS FOR ANIMALS
Description: Injured animals need our help to alleviate their suffering through the technology of 3D printed prosthetics and assistive devices.
Community Partner: The CAP Project (www.thecapproject.org). CAP works with various groups and sanctuaries. Volunteers are matched based on geographical area.
Materials Needed: Varies by project, 3D printer and filament (typically ABS or PLA, though if you choose to help with aquatic birds more exotic filament may be needed). Choose the projects best suited to your printer's capabilities.
Instructions: Those who wish to volunteer with CAP need to fill out a volunteer form located on its website. You will be matched with an animal in need.
Caveat: The matching process may take a week to a month. Programming or planning this activity for a specific timeframe is not practical. Participation with service or youth groups that meet regularly makes more sense.
Doing More: While waiting to be matched, read *Beauty and the Beak: How Science, Technology and a 3D Printed Beak Rescued a Bald Eagle* (Rose & Veltkamp 2017), an inspiring tale of how an illegally shot bald eagle was rescued and rehabilitated through human compassion and 3D technology. Be sure to discuss extinction and environmental conservation efforts with youth.

MAXIMIZING YOUR IMPACT

Supply Drive

While your group gets together to work on animal-based service projects, simultaneously run a collection drive. Most animal shelters need newspapers, towels, and cat and dog food (and possibly small mammal food). Most shelters are always in need of laundry detergent. Some shelters post their needs on their Facebook page for someone in the community to respond. Call or follow your local animal rescue groups to see how your group can further assist their efforts. Be sure to also post your supply needs (fabric, yarn) to social media to allow your teens to make more of difference regardless of your library budget.

In addition to obtaining supplies to donate locally, initiate a Wands for Wildlife (http://www.appalachianwild.org/wands-for-wildlife.html) collection drive. Donate used mascara wands cleaned with soap and water to the Appalachian Wildlife Rescue. The rescue foundation uses the wands to remove debris from various small wildlife during the rehabilitation process. Here's another example of upcyling items instead of throwing them out, benefiting both the environment and wildlife. Ask around, wands could be donated locally to a wildlife rehabilitator in your community.

Education/Learning

Why are there so many abandoned pets? How are animals becoming injured? What else could be done? Allowing youth to analyze and reflect on current situations is advantageous. Each generation has the ability to design and solve a set of problems. As youth leaders, we should encourage this type of thinking among our participants.

6

Hunger, Homelessness, and Shelter

As you grow older, you will discover that you have two hands:
one for helping yourself, the other for helping others.
—Audrey Hepburn

CALENDAR

Here are a few specific related events and celebrations to plan your programming:

National Foster Care Month (May)
Hunger Action Month (September)
Hunger and Homelessness Awareness Week (November)
World Food Day (October 16)
Souper Bowl of Caring (January/February, weeks leading up to the Super Bowl Game)

HUNGER

Hunger, or more specifically food insecurity, in the United States varies from state to state. Food insecurity is the lack of access to food or not enough food for a given household. In the United States, the predominant cause of food insecurity is poverty ("11 Facts about Hunger").

Food Delivery Programs
Project: LUNCH BAGS
Description: In addition to a delivery of a hot meal, food delivery programs often provide a cold meal. This meal can be delivered in decorative lunch bags made by your youth participants.
Community Partners: Local Meals on Wheels or other community food delivery service provider.
Materials Needed: Paper lunch bags, coloring supplies—markers, colored pencils. Any decorative items you have handy, such as stickers.

Instructions: Have youth decorate the lunch bags with beautiful designs or uplifting messages.

Project: PLACEMATS
Description: As part of the food delivery, colorful placemats can be given out to brighten up the meal recipient's day.
Community Partners: Local Meals on Wheels or other community food delivery service provider.
Materials Needed: Use any of the following you have available: Legal size (8½ × 14 inch) white paper, 11 × 17-inch white paper or 12 × 18-inch construction paper, colored pencils, markers, or crayons. Optional: Laminate the placemats for longer use.
Instructions: Have participants decorate the placemats with decorative images, messages, or holiday themes.

Project: OVEN MITTS
Description: Food delivery personnel need to protect their hands from hot containers. Here's a nice way to help a volunteer.
Community Partners: Local Meals on Wheels or other community food delivery service provider. Soup kitchens.
Materials Needed: Solid light-colored oven mitt, Sharpie permanent markers or fabric paint.
Instructions: Place mitt on a flat surface; you may want to put down old newspapers to protect your tables. Allow participants to decorate the mitts using either markers or paint or a combination of both. Allow time to dry particularly if using paint.

Project: LITTLE FREE PANTRY/FOOD EXCHANGE BOX
Description: A recent twist on the community book exchange, or Little Free Library, is a "blessings box" or "yard-based food pantries." Styled like a Little Free Library, the purpose of this community box is to exchange and provide food and personal care items. Strategically placed community boxes are popping up all over towns across the nation (Shaar 2017).
Community Partners: You'll need permission to place your food box on private property. Look to faith-based organizations and civic groups in your neighborhood. Your public library could be a good location as well. If you need help building the box, look to your school woodshop teacher or local carpenters.
Materials Needed: Purchase a kit from the Little Free Library website or build a box yourself. Wood can be upcycled from a school woodshop class or donated by a carpenter or your local chain home improvement store.
Instructions: If you've purchased a kit from the Little Free Book organization, follow the assembly directions and place in a favorable location. Otherwise, obtain instructions for building a structure featuring a generic box with a door and waterproof roof, if located outdoors. In either case, youth can plan the design of your box or just simply paint and seal it. Many of the boxes have themes and chosen color schemes.
Caveat: Some thought and planning need to go into deciding the location of the box particularly if placed on public property. Even on private property, permission and perhaps permits need to be obtained.

Doing More: Youth should be involved in organizing food donations and stocking the pantry on an ongoing basis. They should also actively promote the availability of this service within the community.

HOMELESSNESS

In 2014 in the United States, "on a single night 578,424 people were experiencing homelessness. Of those, 401,051 were sheltered, and 177,373 people experiencing homelessness were unsheltered. Individuals made up 63 percent and people in families were 37 percent" (United States Interagency Council on Homelessness 2015, 16). Whether in a shelter or out in the elements, homeless persons can be aided and comforted by the projects listed below.

Project: WE CARE KITS

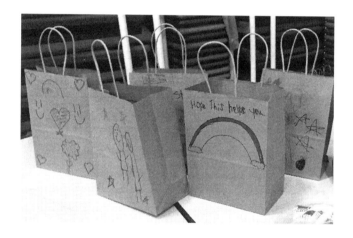

Description: Many organizations collect personal care items to be distributed to the homeless.

Community Partners: Civic and religious groups are great contacts, particularly those with soup kitchens and pantries.

Materials Needed: Plain handled paper shopping bags, crayons, colored pencils, markers in a variety of colors, stickers, or any decorative items you have in your supply. Kits should include some of the following items: toothpaste, toothbrush, dental floss. Local dentist may be willing to donate these items. Local hotels may donate small-size soaps. Deodorant, combs, lip balm, lotion, wet wipes, and tissue packs. Small snacks such as protein bars, jerky or peanut butter, and crackers. Water bottle.

Instructions: Run a collection drive for toiletries and other necessities to put in the We Care Kit bags. To add a caring, personal touch, have youth hand decorate each bag, which allows the recipient to feel special while receiving basic necessities. Decorate each bag with a special, heartfelt message. Fill bags with the items collected. Deliver the kits to your community partner for distribution.

A completed sleep mat.

Project: PLARN SLEEP MATS FOR THE HOMELESS

Materials Needed: 500–700 plastic grocery bags per sleep mat, scissors, crochet hook (size: L or larger): You need a large-size hook, but one that is comfortable in your hands.

Community Partners: Faith-based groups with soup kitchens, homeless shelters, for distribution of mats. Whom to work with making the mats: Community-based organizations dedicated to the environment. Any school club with an emphasis on sustainability and reducing waste would likely want to join in on a project such as this. The task of making the plarn is time consuming. The handles and bottom cut pieces were taken to a local supermarket for recycling.

Instructions to Make Plarn: Collect plastic bags. Lay several bags together: one on top of the other. Cut off the handles and the bottom, and then cut the rest of the bag into strips approximately 2–3 inches in width. This will leave you with plastic circle strips.

Attach the strips together to form a string of plastic (also known as *plarn*). Roll up the plarn into balls (skeins) for use.

Instructions to Crochet Mat: You want a cushiony mat so don't crochet with too much tension. A larger hook also makes it easier to crochet looser. The mat should be approximately 3 × 6 feet. Single chain.

Caveat: You may be concerned that there will no longer be grocery bags available for this project, as some communities have begun to ban these items. Plastic will be available. The plastic from dry cleaning bag covers, the newspaper delivery sleeves and department store bags will continue to be in use. You'll have to compare the length and quantity you can get versus the grocery bags when making this item with plastic from other sources. For thicker plastic bags, cut thinner strips.

Modification: Weaved Plarn Sleep Mat

Instead of crocheting the plarn, youth can weave a mat. You'll need a large loom: one that is 3–4 feet across and approximately 5–6 feet long. You can make your own loom upcycling an old chalkboard frame or attaching four pieces of wood in the desired length and width, then hammer nails at the top and bottom frame an inch apart until the wood is covered. Old picture frames make great individual looms, too!

Modification: Quilted Sleep Mats

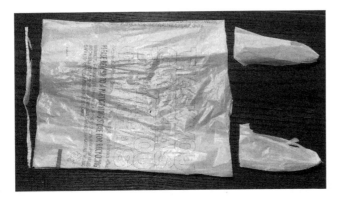

Cut off handles and end.

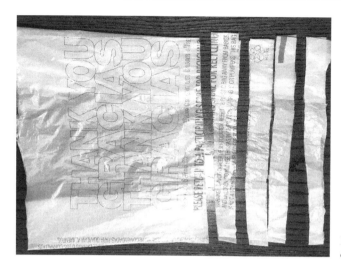

For even strips a rotary cutter can be used.

Connect each strip.

My Brother's Keeper Quilt Group in Pennsylvania has been making sleeping bag quilts for the homeless since 1985. Using scraps of fabric, it pieces together the quilts and deliver them to the homeless (Kim 2016). If you have a sewing group and access to sewing machines, quilted sleeping bags are an option.

Children in Foster Homes and Shelters

Adults are not the only ones who are homeless. Many children live in various temporary housing shelters. Children often arrive in foster homes and shelters with nothing and often when they do have a few items to bring, those items are carried in garbage bags. On your rounds at library conferences, obtain decorative bags from children and young adult book publishers and donate them to local shelters. These make a welcome and cheerful change from garbage bags youth are destined to use in these last-minute emergency situations. The trauma of being removed from an unsafe home, being abandoned or abused, is coupled with the loss of possessions. No special blanket, no stuff animal, and no favorite bag to store them. Organize a collection drive of these items or better yet make them!

Project: NO SEW FLEECE BLANKET

Community Partners: My Stuff Bags Foundation (http://www.mystuffbags.org/)—blankets, handmade items, supplies. Check its website for current needs or partner with a shelter in your area. Blankets made for My Stuff should be single ply to make room for more "stuff" in the child's bag.

Materials Needed: 1¼—1½ yard of fleece 58 inches wide, scissors.

Instructions: My Stuff Bags has a PDF instruction sheet (http://www.mystuffbags.org/how-to-help/make-a-blanket/) for you to duplicate and hand out to participants. Child and teen-size blanket included. Cut a 4 × 4-inch square on each of the four corners and discard. On all four sides of the blanket cut 4 inches long cuts 1 inch apart. Tie an overhand knot midway in each strip.

Project: ENCHANTED MAKEOVERS—BEAUTIFYING SHELTER HOMES

Description: You may also inquire at local shelters in your area to see what your group can provide. In Michigan, Enchanted Makeovers, founded by interior designer Terry Grahl, organizes room makeovers for shelter homes housing women and children. Enchanted Makeovers is in need of sewn pillowcases, twin size quilts, baby quilts, handmade dolls, and capes for kids. Instructions for all these projects are found throughout this book. Crocheted or knitted lap blankets of size 35 × 40 inches are needed, too. Check out its website (http://enchantedmakeovers.org/pages/help.htm) for specific needs and mailing address. If you are able to complete any of these projects, contact Enchanted Makeovers or donate locally to a shelter in your neighborhood. If you prefer to donate locally, make sure you ascertain what is needed first. It's possible some of the projects listed in other chapters would be welcomed, too. Communicate with community partners for the best possible outcome.

Project: CAPES FOR KIDS

Description: Make marginalized children feel like superheroes!

Materials Needed: Approximately 1 yard of fabric per cape, scissors, 1½-inch Velcro, extra fabric or felt for decorative logos and emblems. Optional: Other embellishments.

Community Partners: Enchanted Makeovers, local shelter, hospital pediatric ward.

Instructions: Cape templates available from *Family Fun* (June/July 2016) on Parents.com website (http://www.parents.com/fun/printables/familyfun-printables/) or simply trace out a cape pattern on a solid color washable fabric. Sew on embellishments such as superhero logos. To close the cape at the neck, sew on a 2-inch square of Velcro to each side.

SHELTER

One of the largest organizations dealing with housing and facilitating the acquisition of shelter is Habitat for Humanity. Habitat for Humanity has numerous satellite offices across the country, and many school Habitat for Humanity clubs flourish. Work with your local agency. Call up and ask what they need; you may even be able to "adopt a family." Habitat will give you information on the family's favorite quotes, colors, and even photographs to be used in the wood transfers project below. Everything you do will be personalized to suit your host family.

Habitat is also noted for making critical repairs on homes for veterans. Other organizations helping out veterans include Homes for Our Troops and Building Homes for Heroes. "Veterans made up 11 percent of all adults experiencing homelessness counted on a single night. The number of Veterans experiencing homelessness has been declining rapidly in recent years, as VA and HUD have been actively engaged in working with local public housing authorities, housing and service providers, and partners in the private sector as well as other Federal, state and local government agencies, to achieve the goal of ending Veterans homelessness. HUD's 2014 PIT count reported there were 49,933 Veterans experiencing homelessness" (United States Interagency Council on Homelessness 2015, 26).

Project: WELCOME HOME SIGN

A warm welcome for new homeowners.

Description: Traditionally a Welcome Home sign is given to the family upon moving into a Habitat home.

Materials Needed: Canvas—any size but 21 × 11 inches or other rectangular shape works well, paints and paintbrushes, hardware for picture hanging.

Community Partner: Habitat for Humanity or other home agency in your area.

Instructions: Trace out the words Welcome Home on the canvas. Have youth paint the sign in a variety of complementary colors. Let dry. Affix picture hanging hardware.

Caveat: Call your local Habitat office before you do this project. This is one of its most visible projects and is often undertaken by children of all ages and by numerous service groups. Your local Habitat may be inundated with these signs. It's better to move on to a project that is truly needed or wanted for the most impact on youth participation.

Pleasant quotes add to the home décor.

Project: WOOD TRANSFERS

Description: These unique plaques brighten any home! They're perfect for personalized décor for groups that Adopt-a-Family.

Materials Needed: Wood (approximately 4 × 6-inch pieces), sandpaper, acrylic medium glue, Mod Podge glue (matte or gloss finish), paintbrush or foam brush for spreading the medium and the glue, laser printer and image (see caveats), standard kitchen sponge (4.7 × 3 inches) cut up into eight (1 × 1¼ inches) square pieces (cut lengthwise, then across three times making four pieces each half). Each participant only needs a small square, and these can be shared and reused. Water and a container for the water, for example a cup, bowl, or upcycled plastic yogurt cup. An upcycled plastic gift card, hotel key, or stiff cardboard. Hardware for hanging boards, ribbon optional.

Money Saver: To save money on supplies, ask your school woodshop teacher for leftover wood. They usually have nice size squares and rectangles leftover. If your school does not have a woodshop, ask for donations at your local lumber supply, contractors, or even at the local martial arts dojo.

Community Partners: Habitat for Humanity or other local home agency. In schools, partner with members of the Habitat for Humanity Club.

Instructions: Using an inkjet printer, print an image of your choice. If the image is a quote, you'll need to print a mirror image. Flip the image using photo editing software such as Photoshop or Paint. An image can be flipped in Microsoft Word by clicking on the image. Once highlighted click on the *Format* tab. In the *Arrange* section, locate the *Rotate* menu, click and choose *Flip Horizontal*. This will give you a mirror image. Using sandpaper, sand the wood surface on the front of the board. Brush off any wood dust. Apply a thin coating of acrylic medium using the brush first in one direction then brush in the opposite direction so that the surface is completely coated. Then apply the medium using the same brush to the front of the image completely. Place the image face down on the prepared board. Cover paper with the medium again. Remember, each time a thin coat only. Squeegee any glue from the paper image using a plastic gift card, hotel card key, or thick cardboard (not corrugated) cut to a similar size. Inspect the paper and ensure there are no air bubbles. Repeat until paper is smooth and no air bubbles exist. Allow to dry completely either overnight or under a bathroom hand dryer. It must be completely dry. Next, wet the sponge and apply in a circular motion to the paper on the board. You may also use your finger without the sponge, but most prefer to use the sponge. The paper will begin to wipe away, and the image will be left behind. Keep repeating this step until your board is free of paper pulp and smooth. You'll need to do this several times. Let dry then cover your board with a protective layer of Mod Podge glue to seal. Let dry. Optional: Before the final top coat layer of Mod Podge you may apply color to wash your board, if you wish; otherwise leave it natural looking. Attach hardware for hanging, ribbon optional.

Caveat: You must only use an inkjet printer. Be patient when removing the paper pulp; this is the longest step and the most important.

Project: KEY RING HOLDER

Alternatives: You may do a wood transfer as described above in the project Wood Transfers or you may choose to paint your wood board. A wood transfer of an old-fashioned key or Home Sweet Home saying is a nice option, but more involved. Less involved is mod-podging images on the board and sealing it

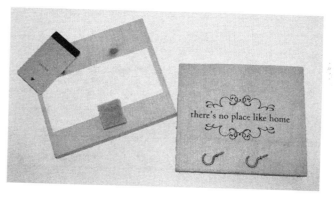

Add hardware to create a key ring holder.

with the glue. Again, images of keys from magazines or any pleasant image such as flowers make a nice touch.

Instructions: Have youth paint the board and stencil the word *Keys* once paint has dried. Attach 3–4 hooks below for hanging keys. Attach hardware in the back of the board for hanging.

Modification: Or, have youth cut out images from an upcycled magazine. Images are glued onto the board using Mod Podge on the back and front. Cover the board completely, then seal with a coat of Mod Podge glue. Let dry.

MAXIMIZING YOUR IMPACT

Supply Drive

Simultaneously run a collection drive while your group gets together to work on service projects. Basic toiletries and necessities are always needed. Food collection drives are easy to arrange with your local food pantry. Youth can decorate collection boxes drawing attention to and advertising the effort.

Education/Learning

What is the local need for food and housing? What are some community resources? How does this compare nationally or globally? Libraries can provide lists of community resources for those who need.

7

Health and Wellness

You're happiest while you're making the greatest contribution.
—Robert F. Kennedy

There is nothing more fundamental than one's health and wellness. Those of us in good health can take care of others and make those less fortunate more comfortable by creating items to lessen suffering and pain. From postsurgical comfort pillows for breast cancer survivors to 3D printed hands for limbless children, the ability to provide assistance is priceless.

CALENDAR

Here are a few specific related events and celebrations to plan your programming:

American Heart Month (February)
Braille Literacy Month (January)
Breast Cancer Awareness Month (October)
Every Kid Healthy Week (April)
Mental Health Month (May)
National Letter Writing Day (December 7)
National Physical Fitness and Sports Month (May)
National Relaxation Day (August 15)
Stress Awareness Month (April)
World Mental Health Day (October)

HEALTH

Encouraging Postcards
Project: POSTCARD PICK ME UP (http://www.postcardpickmeup.org/)
Description: Postcard Pick Me Up campaign impacts patients in hospitals and long-term care facilities by providing a personal token of concern. Children write encouraging get-well wishes for patients who need a "pick me up." Hospital patients can be any age. Schools and public libraries can encourage participation among English language learners

(ELLs). These youth are not only practicing writing in English, but can also write words of encouragement in their native languages. This makes for a more inclusive activity not only for the ELL but also for the recipient who needs that extra personal touch in their language. Many public libraries also have English language classes as part of their programming, and this activity would pair nicely with such programs.

Materials Needed: Gather postcards or make your own from paper using weight stock of 67 lb or higher (67–110); drawing utensils such as colored pencils, crayons, or markers in a variety of colors; stickers.

Community Partner: Postcard Pick Me Up or start your own partnership with local health-care facilities.

Instructions:

- Cut cardstock paper into 4 × 6 inches
- Decorate a postcard
- Write an encouraging note
- Individually address postcards. However, they can be mailed together in one envelope. This gives the receiver the impression of having an individual card
- Mail to Postcard Pick Me Up, or other similar organization

Caveats: No glitter, perfumes, or scents should be added to the cards, as this can affect patients. Also, confirm languages needed or most desired. To make the most impact, contact organizers and query their current needs.

Project: SENDING SMILES (http://www.sendingsmiles2sis.com/)

Description: Sending Smiles' recipients are children, and cards should be decorated and written for this age group. Knock, Knock jokes are a great way to elicit a smile. Leave a list of silly jokes next to the postcards for participants unsure of what to say; it helps them get started. Contact Sending Smiles, and it will send you the postcards free of charge. Included in your package is a self-addressed stamped envelope to mail your written, decorated postcards back for distribution. This is as free as it gets! Sending Smiles partners with health-care facilities such as St. Jude's, in addition to sending cards to individuals. Using this website, you can add the name of a child in need of a smile. Encourage your youth to add classmates and family members in need of a smile, too.

Materials Needed: Drawing utensils, colored pencils, crayons, markers in a variety of colors; stickers, if available. Upcycled decorative mailing labels with the addresses cut off come in handy and are free.

Instructions: Request postcards at www.sendingsmiles2sis.com/. Decorate postcards with jokes, words of encouragement, hand-drawn pictures, or stickers. This allows for creativity among your participants.

Caveat: Depending on age, not all children can read script, so encourage your youth participants to write in print when writing out postcards.

Project: GIRLS LOVE MAIL (http://www.girlslovemail.com/)

Description: Handwritten and decorated notes of encouragement to newly diagnosed women with cancer. Accepts notes written in Spanish, making this an inclusive option for youth with limited proficiency in English.

Instructions: Download its kit at http://www.girlslovemail.com/groups/

Project: HAT PARADE FUND-RAISER

Description: In 2015, Commack Road Elementary School (Islip, NY) hosted its first Hat Parade fund-raiser benefiting the Heavenly Hats organization. Its parade was in honor of the school's former principal diagnosed with cancer. Heavenly Hats provides new hats for cancer patients and others who lose their hair due to certain medical conditions. Participating groups organize a parade and ask participants to donate $1 to march in the parade with a hat of their choice. Typically, students are not allowed to wear hats to school as it is against typical dress

Use LittleBits circuits to spin a varsity letter.

code policies in place. So, for $1 they have the privilege to wear a hat during school hours. This is similar to Wear Red or Jeans to Work programs where employees make a donation to the chosen organization and then participants have the benefit of dressing accordingly. Our students participated in a hat challenge to create hats for our administrators attending the parade. Creations included hats with oversized pom-poms and rotating varsity letters connected to LittleBits circuits. Student imagination was their limit. Glue guns, sewing, wearable technology in the form of circuits lining the hats made a significant contribution to a solemn but joyful event.

Community Partner: Heavenly Hats (http://heavenlyhats.org/), American Cancer Society, local hospitals and health-care facilities can all benefit from the funds raised. Cancer support groups. Alopecia support groups.

Materials Needed: Ask youth to bring a hat to be decorated or use newspapers or cardboard to form a base hat; decorations can be anything you have on hand; you'll need craft glue, glue guns and tape as adhesives.

Instructions: Encourage youth to be creative and use any supplies you have on hand. Hats can be decorated with colorful bottle caps or newspaper flowers! No need to spend extra money on supplies. Upcycle everyday materials. Each hat will be as unique as the participant's personality.

Sewing Projects for Medical/Surgical Patients

Project: COMFORT PILLOWS FOR POST-SURGICAL BREAST CANCER SURVIVORS

Description: Comfort pillow placed under one's armpit alleviates the pain of postsurgical incisions due to mastectomies.

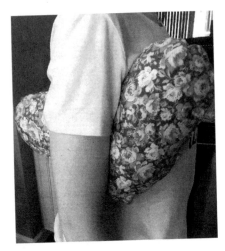

Photo credit: Rita Dockswell

Self-made heart template.
Photo credit: Rita
Dockswell

Community Partners: Hospitals, chemotherapy infusion centers, support groups.
Materials Needed: Fabric, Poly-Fil stuffing, needle and thread, straight pins; can use sewing machine or hand sewn.

- Fabric—choose something very soft as patients use these pillows post surgically and you want the recipient to be as comfortable as possible as they will already have discomfort from their surgical incision.
- Poly-Fil stuffing—but don't overstuff making the pillow hard. Again, aim for soft and comfortable.

Instructions: Make a heart-shaped template; finished heart should be approximately 11½ inches across and 10 inches high. Trace the template on the fabric, then cut out two heart shapes, and face them right-side together. Pin the hearts together. Sew the hearts leaving a 3–4-inch opening. Turn the heart inside out and proceed to stuff with the Poly-Fil. When pillow is sufficiently fluffy, sew the opening closed.
Caveats: Soft fabric, don't overstuff the pillow making it too firm as this will not be comfortable.

Project: PORT PILLOWS
Description: Patient catheters (ports) are placed beneath the skin in the upper chest area of patients receiving long-term medical treatment. These ports are convenient, alleviating the need for needle sticks every time the patient needs a chemotherapy infusion. However, their location across the shoulder right at the seatbelt line makes car rides extremely uncomfortable. Port pillows provide relief and comfort while riding in cars.
Community Partners: Hospitals, chemotherapy infusion centers, support groups.
Materials Needed: Fabric, thread, polyester fiber fill, sewing machine, Velcro (½–⅝ inch).
Instructions: Cut out two rectangles (4 × 7 inches). Cut two pieces of Velcro 3½ inches. Machine baste one side of Velcro to right side of fabric, loop side up. Stitch only one end of Velcro, leaving the other end free. Next, baste other half of Velcro strip to opposite side of fabric, loop side down. Pin the rectangles together and sew right side in with a ¼-inch seam. Leave a 2-inch opening. Turn the pillow right side out and proceed to stuff with the Poly-Fil. When pillow is sufficiently fluffy, sew the opening closed.
Caveat: Use sew-on Velcro, not the adhesive kind.

Project: BLANKETS FOR BABIES—PROJECT LINUS (https://www.projectlinus.org/)
Description: Project Linus is a well-established organization benefiting children. Participants can find numerous free printable patterns on its website. Blankets can be sewn,

no-sew, crocheted, or knitted. This gives you a range of possibilities for entry into this project. Have your teens make blankets for preemies, babies, and children.

Materials Needed: Depending upon the type of blanket pattern chosen. Typically, blankets can be crocheted or knitted. For these you'll need crochet hooks or knitting needles, yarn, and scissors. Fabric blankets are also acceptable. For these blankets you'll need fabric, scissors, needle and thread, or a sewing machine and thread.

Instructions: Choose a pattern from the Project Linus website: http://www.projectlinus .org/patterns/.

Caveats: Blankets should be made in smoke-free and pet-free environments, which should not pose a problem for most libraries. Sick children cannot be exposed to these containments as they are harmful to frail children. Do not include any embellishments that could pose a choking hazard.

Doing More: Run a fabric or yarn drive for your local chapter. Chapters are often in need of blanket-making supplies.

Project: CASES FOR SMILES (http://caseforsmiles.org/)

Description: Patients so small and fragile undergoing countless procedures and treatments. Subjected to separation, isolation, and often painful procedures, being hospitalized and undergoing cancer treatment can be a frightening and traumatic experience for young patients. The founders of Cases for Smiles not only deliver cheerful pillowcases to sick children but are also "developing one of the first initiatives to address pediatric medical post-traumatic stress" ("FAQs" Ryan's Case for Smiles). Each handmade, decorative pillowcase comes with information about post-traumatic stress to help each family.

Community Partners: Cases for Smiles; school Family and Consumer Science teachers and community sewing groups can provide advice and mentorship.

Materials Needed: Cheerful, colorful 100 percent cotton fabric, sewing machine, and cotton thread. Border: ⅓ of a yard of fabric cut into a strip, 10½ × 40½ inches; Case: ¾ of a yard, 26½ × 40½ inches.

Instructions: Follow the directions given in its free PDF "How to Sew a Pillowcase" guide found on the website (http://caseforsmiles.org) or use your favorite pillowcase template; just be sure the pillow measures to standard hospital size. Hospitals use standard-size pillowcases (20 × 26 inches).

Caveat: Website has guidelines prohibiting glitter, flannel, and red-colored fabrics. Be sure to read over their requirements prior to beginning this project. Pillowcases need to be washed in unscented detergent, then ironed and folded into a quart- or gallon-size plastic bag prior to donation. This part of the activity can be done by a volunteer at home or perhaps by someone who would like to participate but cannot sew.

Project: EASY SEW FLEECE CHEMO CAP

Description: Those who lose their hair due to chemotherapy treatments are often cold and need to cover their head. These can also be used for other medical conditions where hair loss is a concern, such as alopecia.

Community Partners: Hospitals, chemotherapy centers, support groups.

Materials Needed: Your favorite beanie-style cap—you will use this as a guide to trace out the cap you'll make; soft fleece fabric, sewing machine, pencil for tracing, scissors, straight pins, and thread.

Instructions: Lay out the fleece two sheets of the fabric one on top of the other. Place the beanie on top of the two layers of fleece and trace along the beanie. Cut out the two layers (sides) of fleece. Trim if needed to make the two sides identical in length and shape. Pin in place and sew around the edges, leaving the bottom open. Lay the cap with the seams running down the middle, then sew around the edges but when you get toward the top of the cap, go across the top of the cap to the other side and down again. Can be embellished with decorative accessories, if desired. Leave the bottom open. Cut off the top of the cap, just above the seam. Turn the cap inside out.

Caveats: While this activity requires a sewing machine, it is an easy straight stitch that all beginners should be able to handle. Buy the softest fleece you can find. The cap will be worn in direct contact with skin of someone who doesn't feel well.

Project: CEREBRAL PALSY BIBS

Description: Cerebral palsy (CP) is a disorder that affects body movement and muscle coordination. People with CP may experience problems with swallowing, including saliva. These bibs help keep the wearer dry.

Community Partners: Your local United Cerebral Palsy affiliate and support groups. We made these bibs for the nephew of one of our staff members. She asked if we could help, so we got out our sewing machines! Projects in this book can help individuals in your neighborhood directly, as well as community organizations.

Materials Needed: 22½ × 22½-inch cotton fabric, 11 × 11-inch washcloth (Money Saver: You can upcycle towels and cut them to size or hold a face cloth donation drive), sewing machine, and thread.

Cut off a corner of the washcloth before sewing.

Instructions:

- Cut your fabric to 22½ × 22½ inches.
- Create a ¼-inch hem on all four sides of the square and sew with a ¼-inch seam allowance.
- Cut off a corner of the washcloth so that when you fold over the fabric it lays flat. Measure each side of one corner of the washcloth to approximately 9 inches and mark. Draw a line straight

across to each mark. Using scissors, cut on the line. You now have a square washcloth with one corner missing.
- Pin the washcloth 1 inch from the corner of the main fabric square, with the straight side on the opposite side of the fabric.
- Sew along the edge of the washcloth with a ¼-inch seam allowance. Use thread that matches the color of your main fabric square.
- Once the washcloth is sewed to the fabric, fold the fabric square in half to make a triangle, covering the washcloth. Pin the fabric in place.
- Topstitch along the edges of the triangle (not the fold) using a ¼-inch seam allowance.
- Iron flat.

Caveat: The measurements are for a child-size bib.

Project Ideas for Nursing Homes

Help your local nursing home or rehabilitation facility by making walker caddies that are sewn and attached with Velcro to a resident's walker to help him or her maintain their independence. People with compromised mobility need their hands to hold on to their walker, and this condition limits one's ability to carry personal items such as a book, phone, or newspaper. Makers need to know how to use a sewing machine to make walker caddies. For a simpler project, throw pillows can brighten a resident's room. Square pillows require an easy straight stitch on a sewing machine that can be mastered by most youth. Call your local nursing homes facility to inquire what types of donations they will accept and what they prefer. This is an opportunity to match your students' talent with the needs of a community facility.

Project: ALZHEIMER'S ACTIVITY MAT
Description: Helps with memory, attention, and focus. Stimulates the senses and provides exercise for muscles of the hand.
Materials Needed: Fabric, zipper, pockets, buttons, snaps, and so on; needle and thread; scissors.
Instructions: You can upcycle a fabric placemat as your starting point or choose to make one. Then sew on various devices such as zippers and snaps. Create pockets and loops from fabric scraps and sew to the placemat.
Money Saver: Upcycle zippers, buttons, and the like from a clothing collection drive. You're only limited by your supplies.

Project: ALZHEIMER'S MEMORY BOX
Description: While attending a National Youth Leadership Council Service Learning conference, on display was an exhibit where students had made Memory Boxes for those afflicted with Alzheimer's disease. It was part of the biography curriculum, where students wrote a report on a local individual or family member. As part of the project, they also made a diorama shadow box filled with items related to the individual's life. The students related that some of those afflicted with this disease upon seeing the box became animated and quite talkative relating the details of their lives. While this is not a medical intervention, it was anecdotally a positive experience for all involved.
Community Partners: Nursing homes, assisted living facilities, and support groups. Youth may be inspired to create a box for a family member.
Materials Needed: Upcycled shoe boxes. You'll need items unique to the recipient's life story (see instructions).

Instructions: You'll need to contact a community partner for access and protocol for speaking with Alzheimer's patients and their families. Alternatively, you can run this as programming for youth with family members diagnosed with Alzheimer's. Youth will need to interview the Alzheimer's patient and possibly their families to gather key points of the recipient's life. Some of the information can be researched such as popular songs and movies of a given decade. Other details such as the recipient's first car or military service can be represented by an upcycled toy car or picture. The idea is to give the recipient of the box a visual to spark past memories and encourage communication.

Knitting and Crocheting for Medical/Surgical Patients

An incredible example of the value of traditional crafting skills being used to save lives can be found in Bolivia. Aymara women, known for their distinctive knitting and weaving craftwork, are weaving medical devices for children born with heart defects. Using elastic metal known as nitinol, the women weave devices that close up a congenital hole in the heart (de los Reyes, 2015). Running library programs that teach our next generation to knit, sew, or weave may have unintended benefits, namely, making the world a better place.

Project: PICC LINE BANDAGE COVER
Description: PICC stands for peripherally inserted central catheter. It is an intravenous

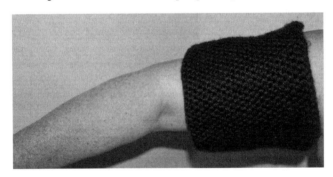

(IV) line inserted into the patient's arm just below the shoulder and above the elbow. It allows medical professionals to administer large doses of antibiotics to the patient. PICC is also known as a central line.
Community Partners: Hospitals, support groups.
Materials Needed: Crochet hook size E, yarn, scissors.

Instructions: PICC lines are used for both children and adult patients.

Child size: Chain 30 plus one for turning. Starting in the second chain from the hook, single crochet into each loop. Chain 1, turn. Single crochet into the back loop of each stitch. Repeat until you have a piece that unstretched is 6 inches long. Cut yarn leaving about a 10 inch tail. Sew closed lengthways carefully, being sure to not make bumps. Weave in ends.

Adult size: Chain 36 plus 1 for turning. Make as child size except make the piece 8 to 9 inches long unstretched.

Caveats: Gauge is approximately four stitches per inch.
Modifications: If you prefer a fancier pattern and have youth who are more accomplished than a single chain, take a look at Knots of Love patterns (http://www.knotsoflove.org/patterns). It has easy-to-print PDF files for you to use in your endeavor.

Project: WARM UP AMERICA CROCHETED (OR KNITTED) BLANKETS (http://www.warmupamerica.org/)

Description: Blankets squares, or completed afghans, are donated to Warm Up America's partners in hospitals, shelters, hospices, and other social services agencies.

Community Partners: Warm Up America (always check the "Current Needs" tab on its website).

Materials Needed: Yarn, Crochet hooks, knitting needles, scissors.

Instructions: Crochet or knit 7 × 9- inch rectangles. You can send Warm Up America the rectangles made by your group or save them some time and piece the rectangles together to form an afghan. Mail to Warm Up America.

Project: CROCHETED OC-TOPUS FOR PREMATURE BABIES (aka The Danish Octo Project—https://www.sprutte gruppen.dk/danish-octo-project-english/)

Description: Crocheted tentacles remind the newborn of their umbilical cord and of being inside their mother's womb. Danish studies have shown that the octopi kept the babies calm, lessened pulling on their monitors and tubes, and led to better breathing, more regular

Tentacles soothe premature babies.

heartbeats, and higher levels of oxygen in their blood (Rice 2017).

Community Partners: Call your local hospital and ask to speak with someone in charge of the neonatal intensive care unit (NICU). This project is dependent upon approval of NICU/hospital staff. You could also contact local support groups (families of premature infants) to query interest.

Materials Needed: 100 percent cotton yarn, any color; crochet hook (size D or E); washable fiber filling able to withstand 140 degrees Fahrenheit.

Instructions: Patterns are found online at the Danish Octo Project/Spruttegruppen https://www.spruttegruppen.dk/recipes/. Instructions are available in British English, Danish, Italian, Portuguese, and Spanish.

Caveat: For safety, octopi tentacles should be no longer than 8½ inches when stretched out and made of 100 percent cotton yarn able to withstand high temperature washing as all items in contact with premature infants need to be sanitized to prevent infection.

Project: RED CROSS CARDS

Description: Make thank-you cards for blood donors to be given out at upcoming blood drive or make holiday cards for service members and veterans for the Holiday Mail for Heroes campaign.

Community Partners: Local Red Cross chapter, school Red Cross Youth Club.

Materials Needed: Cardstock paper in various colors, markers, colored pencils, stickers, cutout shapes, stamp pad and stamps, or whatever supplies you have access to.

Instructions: Decorate cardstock with positive messages.

Doing More: Host a Blood Drive at your library!

Fill bags with emergency supplies. Photo credit: Rita Dockswell

Project: EMERGENCY "GO BAG"

Description: Every family should have a bag filled with necessities in case of an emergency.

Community Partners: Local Red Cross, officials from town, police, and fire departments.

Materials Needed: Upcycled T-shirts, scissors; beads, optional.

Instructions: This is a no-sew activity. Lay the shirt flat on a table. Cut the sleeves off the T-shirt, and then cut the neckline in a U shape. At the bottom of the shirt, cut ½-inch wide strips 1–2 inches long. Shirt inside out first for no fringe bag. The fringe on the outside is decorated and is a personal preference. Some youth like to add decorative beads to the fringes. There are numerous simple bags to sew if that is preferable. Youth will go home and fill their bags with necessary emergency supplies as instructed by emergency personnel.

Doing More: Host a preparedness fair at your school or library. Invite local Red Cross chapter, fire department, police department, local officials, school security, and health officers. Have stations where youth can put together first aid kits and a preparedness plan. Make a difference in an emergency by being prepared.

Autism/Sensory Toys and Devices

Project: AUTISM CATERPILLAR

Description: These sensory toys are soothing to the autistic child and used by organizations and schools who work with autistic children.

Community Partners: Schools serving autistic children, support groups.

Materials Needed: Fleece or fabric cut to 42 × 12 inches for one caterpillar (a standard bolt [58 × 48 inches] will yield five caterpillars), lentil beans, scissors, needle and thread, ribbon.

Instructions: Sew edges of fleece together lengthwise and one end. At the open end, pour beans in until full using a funnel or a plastic cup as a funnel. Using ribbon, tie off the end tightly—don't let the beans escape! Tie the ribbon, then add a dot of glue, and tie again. Don't use too much glue, as you'll make a mess on the fabric. Lay the caterpillar on a table spreading out the beans evenly so no clumping occurs. Using a wide ribbon (1–1½ inch wide) place approximately 6 inches from the top creating the head portion of the caterpillar. Place six thinner ribbons (¼–½ inch wide) at even intervals of the remaining length. Tie off the big ribbon at the head, add a drop of glue, and then make a pretty bow. Tie off the remaining ribbons with a dot of glue on the knot and then tie a second time. Trim any ribbon so that there's only 1½ inches on either side. Eyes can either be sewn on using a circle of white fabric under a circle of a darker color fabric (upcycle scraps for this), or eyes can be drawn on using a marker.

Caveats: Fabric can be used but the fleece is sturdier to support the weight of the beans and it's soft. It's weight that is needed in this project, so don't substitute beans for lighter materials.

Project: SOCK SNAKE WEIGHTED LAP BELT
Description: The weight and pressure on a child's leg provides physical stimulation that alleviates the need to fidget and bounce legs.
Community Partners: Schools serving autistic children, support groups.
Materials Needed: Long tube-style sock, rice (approximately 8 cups) or beans, needle and thread; essential oil, if desired.
Instructions: Fill the sock with rice using a funnel, plastic cup, or scoop. Sew the top of the sock closed. You may want to do this twice to ensure security and contents won't escape. A soothing essential oil, such as lavender, can be added to the rice prior to filling the sock. For children who tend to pick, use a Sharpie marker, and draw eyes on your snake. Or, you can sew on eyes made of buttons or fabric, if desired.
Caveat: Check with the community partner to assure this item is welcomed.
Modification: Rice socks with essential oils can be microwaved and used as a soothing heating pad around neck, making it a nice gift. Use caution when heating socks; you want warm not burning hot. You'll fill the sock with less rice as you're not looking to add weight around neck.

Project: NO-SEW WEIGHTED BLANKET USING DUCT TAPE
Description: Weighted blankets can be expensive and not affordable for all special needs families.
Community Partners: Schools serving autistic children, support groups. Make these blankets for

Line up rice bags in a row and cover completely with duct tape.

families, and consult with autism agencies to distribute the blankets to families in need.
Materials Needed: For one 5-lb blanket: 5 lb rice or beans, 9 sandwich-size zipper top plastic storage bag, 2 rolls of duct tape, scissors.
Money Saver: Save money by asking food pantries or grocery stores for expired rice or beans. You'll be using these products as weights and not for consumption. Write to tape companies and ask for free duct tape.
Instructions: You'll need to work on a large flat surface such as a table. After filling 9 plastic bags with 1¼ cup of rice, close each bag and lay out bags on a table in 3 rows of 3 bags. Start with four strips of duct tape approximately 24–30 inches long and lay them between the rows of rice, including top and bottom. The width of blanket is your preference; decide how wide you want the blanket when spacing out the plastic bags. Fold over the zipper portion of the plastic bag; the zipper portion should be pressed into the tape centered top to bottom. Then space the remaining two bags across the length of the tape. Affix the bottom of each bag to the next strip of tape at the center of the width (top to

bottom); this leaves room for the next line of bags. Repeat these steps until all rows are complete. Cover the rows with tape on top and around the edges to form a frame. Then apply strips of tape to cover the bags completely using either horizontal or vertical strips. Flip the blanket over and apply tape strips to the backside. Cover any holes and smooth out any edges. Your blanket is now complete.

Note: Typically, the blankets are 10 percent of the child's body weight plus 1 lb. For example, a 40-lb child would need a 5-lb blanket.

Modification: Lap pad. If you want to make just a lap pad, make only one row.

Caveat: Some children may not like the feel of the duct tape. If so, the blanket can be placed inside a pillowcase or a cover can be sewn. Both the pillowcase and tape may be wiped off and cleaned; a nice bonus. Not recommended for children with an oral fixation. Be sure to consult with your partner agency to decide which projects are best suited to its client's needs.

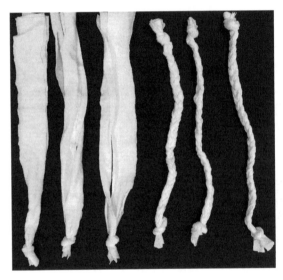

Project: CHEW NECKLACE/ DIY CHEWLERY

Description: Many children on the autism spectrum have an oral fixation; they need to have something in their mouths. Chew necklaces, or chewlery, are available for sale but not all families can afford the many items and services needed for their special needs child. Bonus: These necklaces can be washed.

Community Partners: Support groups for families of autistic children.

Materials Needed: Upcycled T-shirts, scissors.

Instructions: Cut up T-shirts into thin strips 25–30 inches long. Using three strips, tie a knot on one end and then braid the strips together, tying a knot when done. Tie both ends together, and you have a necklace.

Modification: The necklace can be wrapped around a child's wrist several times to make a bracelet.

Caveat: Necklaces pose a choking hazard and should not be distributed to very young children.

Project: CHEW BRACELET

Description: For children with an oral fixation, namely those on the spectrum.

Community Partners: Support groups for families of autistic children.

Materials Needed: Fabric, sewing machine, thread, scissors, straight pin.

Instructions: Cut scraps of fabric into strips 2 × 12 inches. Sew the three strips together at one end. Loosely braid the strands—this allows the fabric to stretch and slide onto a child's wrist. Pin and sew both ends together. This project requires minimal sewing experience.

Blind and Visually Impaired

Project: SENSORY TOUCH BOOK

Description: It can be used with many special needs populations from autistic spectrum to visually impaired as a sensory tool.

Community Partner: Preschool programs for the visually impaired or autistic children, agencies who will distribute to families of special needs children.

Materials Needed: Thick cardstock or preferably cardboard cut to approximately 5 × 6 inches, hole punch, 2–3-inch loose-leaf binder rings, glue, permanent marker. Sensory items can include the following: buttons, feather, bubble wrap, sandpaper, various fabrics such as leather, velvet, corduroy, or fleece, pom-poms, sponge, really whatever you have available to use or can upcycle.

Instructions: Glue each textured item onto a page. Label the item on each page using a marker. Use a hole punch to create holes on the page and then attach the binder rings.

Inclusive Modifications: Remember, the labels can be in English or any language needed if using this book with children on the autism spectrum. For visually impaired youth, you can add Braille.

Project: PLAYDOUGH BRAILLE CELLS

Description: This project is used to teach visually impaired children the six-dot configuration used in Braille. Braille is a tactile representation of letters and words used by the visually impaired and blind to read and communicate. Young sight-impaired children need practice learning the positions of Braille dots when learning the Braille alphabet. They also need to build hand and finger strength by exercising these muscles. The six-well tray filled with balls of dough mimic the six-dot Braille configurations, albeit on a larger scale.

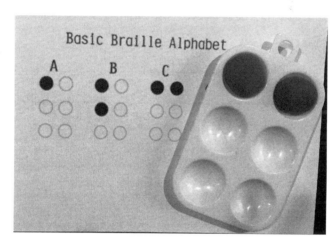

Playdough Braille cells help the visually impaired learn the Braille alphabet.

Materials Needed: Handmade dough (you'll need measuring cups, spoons and mixing bowls and the ingredients listed below), six-well plastic artist palette, plastic storage bags to store dough.

Instructions: Make your favorite playdough recipe or try this aromatic version that smells wonderful. The recipients might not be able to see the bright, beautiful colors, but they can have an alternative sensory experience. Be sure to check with your partner agency which version, scented or unscented, it prefers prior to beginning this project.

Sensory Playdough Recipe (makes 1¾ cups of dough):
1 cup of flour
½ cup salt

2 tbsp cream of tartar
1 tbsp oil
1 cup hot water
1 Kool-Aid packet, any flavor/color (0.13–0.23 oz)

Instructions: Mix flour, salt, Kool-Aid, and cream of tartar together in a bowl. Boil water; this can be done in an electric tea kettle or microwave, whichever your library has available. Mix hot water and oil into the bowl with the dry ingredients. Mix until cool enough to knead. Knead until color is blended. Store in an airtight bag or in a plastic food container. Your partner agency will use the dough to mimic the six-dot Braille configurations. The dough sits in the well depicting a letter of the alphabet. Once a letter is learned, the dough can be reconfigured in the wells to represent the next letter, until all letters are mastered.

Project: 3D PRINTED BRAILLE KEYCHAINS
Description: A librarian in Texas had students design motivational Braille keychains in Tinkercad and then printed them out after her library assistant's husband suddenly lost his sight. Remember, once your colleagues, youth, and community know about your program and commitment to service, ideas will present themselves based on individual needs. Remain open and flexible to new opportunities.
Materials Needed: 3D printer, filament, and key rings.
Instructions: Your youth can print keychains with the words, such as house or files, as a way of helping a visually impaired person keep track of his or her keys by labeling them, or as above, motivational messages. Consult open source files on sites such as Thingiverse (https://www.thingiverse.com/) or Tinkercad (https://www.tinkercad.com/) for ideas and have your group modify files as needed.

Project: 3D PRINTED BRAILLE PUZZLES
Description: The Fittle puzzles are the shape of the item being spelled out in Braille. For example, the fish-shaped puzzle is printed in four pieces; each piece has the next Braille letter so that if you put the puzzle together properly (in letter order) the word f-i-s-h can be read. For beginning readers, this is helpful as they also can feel the overall shape of the item, such as the shape of a fish. For more ideas, consult the Fittle designs (www.thingiverse.com/Fittle/designs) or search Thingiverse. Indeed, typing "Braille" into Thingiverse's search bar will yield numerous projects, from Braille Rubiks Cubes to a Fraction Learning Kit with Braille.
Materials Needed: 3D printer, filament (usually specified on the website) and open-source files, such as those from Fittle, an Indian-based company, on Thingiverse (https://www.thingiverse.com/).
Instructions: Choose a Fittle design (www.thingiverse.com/Fittle/designs) and take a print out.

Project: TACTILE PICTURE BOOKS: BUILD A BETTER BOOK INITIATIVE
Description: Opportunity to develop your own partnership with your local agency for the visually impaired, university mentors, high schools, and public libraries. The University of Colorado at Boulder has partnered with several local public libraries in an effort to have youth 3D print tactile books for visually impaired children. The success of this program inspires others to duplicate it within their communities. Art, literature, and technology come together in this dynamic project. Picture books lose something in the story when there are no pictures. This collaboration includes the Department of Computer Science

and School of Education, several public libraries, and the Colorado Center for the Blind. Tactile Picture Books Project is open to youth in middle school and high school who "design and create accessible, multi-modal picture books that you can see, touch and hear" (http://sciencediscovery.colorado.edu/program/buildabetterbook/).

Visually impaired children don't begin to learn Braille until age six. The availability of 3D tactile children's books means these children can interact with books and engage in reading activities earlier. The group at University of Colorado strives "to better understand the needs of visually impaired toddlers and how parents can effectively engage them in reading." "Equal accessibility to books, offer[s] the whole family a way to experience the magic of reading together" (University of Colorado Boulder 2014).

Instructions: Use Makerbot's Thingiverse, an online community of 3D shareable plans for printed items. Those interested in printing for the visually impaired can search using terms such as Braille, tactile, or visually impaired. Choose a file and print.

More 3D Printed Ideas for the Visually Impaired

Teen students at Dodonaia High School and 7th High School in Ioannina, Greece, designed and created numerous items for the visually impaired using the 3D design platform, Tinkercad. They designed 17 items and the majority of items were printed and are functional: a cup with Braille "Drink Me" inscribed in Braille, academic models including a water molecule, our planetary system, a local city castle, a Braille stamp that translates to conventional language and fun items such as a 3D comic book, Sudoku, and a Rubik's cube in Braille. It should be noted the water molecule with Braille letters on the oxygen and hydrogen molecules was designed and created by a dyslexic student, emphasizing all maker activities and participation in projects be welcoming and inclusive (Kostakis, Niaros, & Giotitsas 2015).

Community Partners: Schools and agencies working with the visually impaired, local visually impaired persons needing these items.

Materials Needed: 3D printer, filament, open-source files.

Instructions: Choose a file from an open source platform such as Thingiverse or Tinkercad or design your own items.

National Challenges for Youth

Your library can host a Hacker Challenge in which you ask your teens to design (and print) an item to benefit the visually impaired or perhaps any service challenge. Or, you can encourage your group to join an established challenge, such as the "Envision the Future Design Challenge" or "Within Reach 3D Design Challenge." MatterHackers, enablingthefuture.org, and Pinshape put out yearly challenges. In 2016, there was the Within Reach Challenge encouraging the design of assistive devices for those without use of their hands and followed up in 2017 with the Envision the Future Design Challenge to encourage design and creation of devices for the visually impaired.

Materials Needed: 3D printer, filament.

Instructions: Follow the specific directions to participate in any one of the challenges listed above.

3D Printing

Project: PROSTHETIC KIDS HAND CHALLENGE AND eNABLE HANDS

Community Partners: Hand Challenge, Project eNable, or design a limb for someone in your community.

Materials Needed: 3D printer, filament, open-source file for prosthetic limb; assembly kit.

Instructions: Sign up at www.handchallenge.com. Tutorial videos for printing hands and troubleshooting tips are given. Videos for assembling hands and assembly kits are available to make this process easier. Follow the step-by-step directions available on the site. Step–by-step instructions are available for the eNable hands at http://enablingthefuture.org/. This site lists more designs for hands, limbs, and other assistive devices.

Modifications: Check out the Facebook group, Amp-Up Amputees. Members of this group print prosthetic superhero arms for kids. Children can sport an Iron Man prosthetic or be Captain America!

Project: IV AND CHEMOTHERAPY BAG COVERS FOR PEDIATRIC PATIENTS

Description: For a child, the hospital can be a frightening place. Couple that with the knowledge that you have a life-altering medical condition requiring hours of intravenous medication. Why not make a child's hospital stay more comfortable by providing IV/chemotherapy bag covers? Whether offering *superhero serum* or *superpower juice*, this is a fun, cute way to empower a small child facing life's harsh realities. This activity could be coupled with sewing groups making matching superhero capes.

Community Partners: Hospitals, infusion centers, home care agencies providing infusions.

Materials Needed: 3D printer, filament.

Instructions: Open-source bag cover file to be downloaded.

Caveat: Call your local hospitals or infusion centers to ensure they will accept this type of donation prior to printing and if they have special requests regarding design. This is not an item that can be dropped off and accepted anywhere. Hospitals have very specific protocol for items coming in contact with extremely ill patients. Some filaments are not compatible with the sterilization process.

Project: 3D PRINTED TICK REMOVER

Description: In certain areas of the country, ticks are prevalent and they cause a variety of debilitating tick-borne diseases. Ticks need to be removed completely and as quickly as possible. This item can be used on humans and animals.

Community Partners: Medical professionals, schools, town vector control personnel, wildlife and hiking groups.

Materials Needed: 3D printer, filament, open-source file such as Tick Twister on Thingiverse (http://www.cel-robox.com/tick-twister/).

Instructions: Access Tick Twister file on Thingiverse and download. Print the tick removal devices. Host an awareness night and hand out the devices, instructions for use (found on Thingiverse), and a general information sheet.

Tip: Ticks are most active during the spring, summer, and early fall months, so plan your event for late winter or early spring.

WELLNESS (MENTAL AND PHYSICAL)

Mental Health

Project: POSITIVE PENCILS

Description: Youth need a reminder that they are special and they are loved!

Community Partner: Distribute these pencils at libraries.

Materials Needed: Standard yellow no. 2 pencils, black Sharpies or in varying colors, if desired.

Instructions: Using the Internet, have youth search for a list of positive affirmations or positive sayings. Youth can come up with their own sayings. Examples: Positive saying:

You are special. Positive affirmation: My dreams are achievable.

Have youth write the positive affirmations or positive sayings along the side of the pencil using a fine-tip Sharpie marker. Let dry a minute or two so the words do not smudge. Pencils can be distributed, left at the reference desk, or you can let your group decide where to place them.

Caveat: Using a fine-tip Sharpie marker will be easier for youth. While this is not a difficult project, some youth might have difficulty writing neatly and clearly in small font on the side of a pencil.

Project: I FOUND A QUILTED HEART

Description: Make hearts using any fabrics and decorations. Attach a note and leave in a random spot to be found by a random person passing by. Hearts are not made for someone; they are left to be found and to make the recipient feel good. This is an anonymous project. The recipient then goes online to say where they found the heart. Not all found hearts are posted, but it is fun to follow. No fees to participate, just the cost of supplies. Hearts are small, so fabric scraps could be used to cut down on costs. Included on the heart is a tag listing the website www.ifoundaquiltedheart .com and a note that says, "I Need a Home."

Plan this activity around Random Acts of Kindness Day (February 17), Random Acts of Kindness Week, or anytime you want to show a kindness!

Community Partner: IFoundAQuiltedHeart.com.

Materials Needed:

- Fabric (scraps are perfect)
- Needle and thread
- Paper for note tag
- Ribbons, buttons, or other decorative items are optional
- Printable participant guidelines and tags can be found at www.ifoundaquiltedheart.com/ participatingintheproject/

Instructions: Lay fabric on flat surface. Cut out heart shape. If you use pinking shears, the edges will be decorative and the hearts will not have frayed edges. Either way, sew the two hearts together leaving a small opening to insert Poly-Fil stuffing. You can use the scrap pieces of leftover fabric if you don't have Poly-Fil. Sew on a ribbon so heart can be hung. Attach a "You Are Loved" or "I Need a Home" message on the heart. These can be handwritten or printed out from the I Found a Quilted Heart website. Each heart will be unique. Provide participants with guidelines on where to place their hearts for others to find.

Caveats: You may leave your heart in any public place where it will be found with the following exceptions: Do not leave hearts at airports as homeland security will not be pleased! Also, do not leave in national parks, as this is against federal regulations against abandoning property. Additionally, it's wise not to leave hearts in public areas where they may be thrown out by cleaning staff or in retail stores where they may be mistaken as merchandise for sale.

Worry doll.

Project: WORRY DOLLS
Description: Young people have many concerns and although a worry doll may not remove these fears, it may alleviate stress. It's good to talk to someone about your troubles and concerns. These small dolls are eager listeners awaiting your worries. Placed under the child's pillow children awake worry free—or so the legend goes. These are pocket-sized dolls and can be kept close at hand for those who need someone to share their worries with during the day.

Community   Partners: School psychologist, social worker. Support groups for children.

Materials Needed: Pipe cleaners, assorted yarn, scissors, wooden or plastic beads.

Instructions: Cut a pipe cleaner in two with one part longer than the other (approximately ⅔ and ⅓). The longer part will be the body and the smaller will be the arms. Make hair by wrapping yarn around your hand several times. Remove. Bend the longer pipe cleaner in half. Center the "hair" between the fold. Slide a bead up the two ends of the long, bent pipe cleaner and thereby attaching the hair and making a head. Fluff the hair. Attach the arms (shorter pipe cleaner) around the body. Draw a face on the bead with a Sharpie marker if desired. Wrap yarn tightly around the legs, body, and arms of the doll. Tie off the yarn to form a knot. You may need or want to trim the hair with a pair of scissors.

Project: GRATITUDE JOURNAL
Description: Reflection journals provide an outlet for our thoughts and concerns and many journal keepers find comfort in this. A gratitude journal focuses solely on positive

feelings by listing five things you're grateful for each day. Listed are good events, experiences, persons, or things in your life.

Community Partners: School psychologist or social worker; educators who promote mindfulness in education.

Materials Needed: Marble notebook (hard-covered with lined pages), Mod Podge craft glue, scissors, paintbrush or foam brush, and assortment of upcycled magazines.

Assorted images chosen from upcycled magazines.

Instructions: Participants will cut out images they find pleasing from the magazines provided. Spread glue on the cover of notebook and affix cut out images. Apply a thin coat of craft glue on top of the images and let dry. Repeat on back cover. Participants take the journals home for self-use.

Project: ART JOURNALS
Description: Some youth can write down their feelings in a writing journal, and some may need an alternative creative outlet to express themselves.

Community Partners: School therapists or local art therapists.

Materials Needed: You can Mod Podge an unlined notebook as described above in Project: Gratitude Journal. However, most notebooks are lined so make books using a binding machine and upcycled

Use either binding combs or binder rings to make art journals.

cookie and cereal boxes. For this you'll need binding machine and binding combs, upcycled cereal and cookie boxes, plain white copier paper, scissors.

Instructions: Cut out a top and bottom cover from your selection of upcycled boxes and paper to size if not making books 8½ × 11 inches. You'll have to cut the binding combs, too, if making smaller sizes. It is simplest to make a standard-size book. Follow directions for your binding machine.

Modifications: If you don't have a binding machine, use a three-hole punch and 2-inch binder rings to create a book.

Art in Health-Care Facilities
Project: PAINTED CEILING TILES FOR RELAXATION AND WELLNESS
Description: Many procedures require patients to remain reclined on exam tables in somewhat generic or sterile surroundings, which can leave patients feeling stressed and uncomfortable. Art students at Biglerville High School created artwork that was installed in exam rooms at the WellSpan Women's Center and Imaging Center located on the Apple Hill Health Campus in York, Pennsylvania. The paintings, which were created on ceiling tiles, were hung on the ceilings of exam rooms at the facility giving patients a pleasant view as opposed to generic white ceiling tiles. Health-care providers at the center use the artwork as icebreakers as voiced by one of the technicians, "the patients will start a conversation about it, and are delighted when they find out a local student painted it." Putting patients at ease is a priority among health-care workers. "Not only [it] improves the patient experience, but enables some budding artists to showcase their talents" ("Young Artists Create" 2016). The art teacher, Lisa Harman, stated, "My students were very excited to know that their art would make someone smile in an otherwise gloomy situation" (personal e-mail, November 29, 2016). Overall, patients get a better view, while health-care providers have an instant talking point that relaxes and distracts patients in a stressful situation.

Community Partners: Start really local, your school health office! Then consider partnering with health-care providers in your community. This project requires communication and partnership. The receiving group has to approve the donation, you must investigate the correct size ceiling tile, and this must conform to local fire safety legislation in your area. Do not present anyone with a "surprise" donation. Contact your local hospital or health-care facility and inquire if they'd like their ceiling tiles painted. Their maintenance staff will supply your group with the tiles.

Materials Needed: Ceiling tiles, acrylic paint, paintbrushes. Drop cloth or newspapers to protect surfaces while painting and making for an easier cleanup.

Instructions: All you need to do is have your group paint cheerful or soothing images on the tiles, allow them to dry, then return the ceiling tiles to the facility. Ask children to paint relaxing, pleasant scenes on the ceiling tiles. Allow time to dry and then donate the tiles to a health-care provider.

Caveat: You need to obtain permission from the school principal (if in a school setting) and from either (or both) the grounds and building supervisor of the facility and your town fire marshal. There may be laws and building codes that could prohibit this activity. Be sure to inquire first. Building codes in medical facilities may differ.

Project: BEADS OF COURAGE—BEADS (http://www.beadsofcourage.org/)
Description: The Beads of Courage program provides children with serious illnesses and their families with a unique way of coping. Through artistic expression, this encouragement program supports the patient, siblings, and clinicians. Beads are given out at various milestones in this arts-in-medicine program. There are certain types of beads they need, so decide which ones are doable with your group. For example, the Acts of Courage Beads glass beads require a kiln and skill to complete. If your library can partner with a local

artist or school with this equipment and staff with the knowledge set, accomplish this task. If not, there are other beads to make such as polymer clay beads.

Community Partners: Beads of Courage organization. Art teachers can provide assistance.

Materials Needed: Bead donation form found on website; preferred hole size is 3/32 inches with no sharp corners, edges, or protrusions; polymer clay in various colors; hard surface to work on, such as a tile; flat blade or craft knife; toothpicks or bamboo skewer to make holes; parchment paper; 400-grit sandpaper; access to oven or toaster oven.

Instructions: Create a long strip of clay to make a pencil-like shape. Refrigerate the beads for 10–15 minutes; this will make it easier to make holes in them. Using a toothpick or skewer, pierce a hole in the bead. Be sure the hole is clear of any residual clay. It's now time to bake the beads. Place beads on a tray lined with parchment paper and bake according to the manufacturer's instructions. Allow beads to cool prior to handling them. Using sandpaper, remove any blemishes or protrusions. Pack up beads, fill out donation form, enclose both in a box, and ship to Beads of Courage. This is a simple, one-color instruction for making one-color simple beads. Depending on the talent and creativity of your group you can investigate polymer bead tutorials on the Internet and make multicolor, unique items. Some of your youth may already be familiar and comfortable using polymer clay and can serve as mentors to others in the group.

Caveat: These beads are worn by children and thus should be sturdy and safe with smooth edges. Use caution when using ovens. Beads will be hot! Do not handle until they are cool.

Project: BEADS OF COURAGE—BEAD BAGS

Description: Now that you've made beads, make some storage bags for them!

Materials Needed: 9 × 12-inch pieces of fabric per bag (2), 26-inch pieces of cording for drawstrings (2), sewing machine, thread, scissors. PDF instructions are available on the Beads of Courage website (http://www.beadsofcourage.org/pages/beadbags.html).

Community Partner: Beads of Courage, sewing instructor, though sewing level is easy.

Instructions: Gather your supplies, as per Beads of Courage instructions, and sew two pieces of 9 × 12-inch fabric together forming a tube approximately 2 inches from the top of the bag for the drawstring to be inserted. Smaller bags can be made using 7 × 10-inch pieces of fabric and 17 inches of cording.

Physical Health
Exercise Equipment

Encourage wellness among school-age children by making and distributing exercise equipment. Physical activity is important at any age but it's good to start the habit early for a long, healthy life. After making the equipment, distribute it to children, donate it to a school for PE classes or recess, or donate it to a daycare or afterschool care facility. Being active and physically fit increases health and wellness.

Project: PLASTIC JUMP ROPES

Description: Jumping benefits cardiovascular health, increases balance, promotes fitness, tones muscles,

Plastic bags are looped together.

burns calories, while providing free exercise equipment and decreasing waste in our landfills.

Community Partners: You can partner with local schools, afterschool care, daycare, and other youth-orientated programs. Many schools participate in Jump Rope for Heart fund-raising events. This is a good way to have extra jump ropes on hand.

Materials: Plastic bags, scissors, duct tape.

Instructions: Lay bags flat on a table. Cut the handles and bottom seam off. You'll now have a plastic circle. Do this to 7–9 bags; length will depend on your preference and the age and height of the children receiving the ropes. Loop the bags together by laying one circle on the other. Pull the top ring under and the bottom ring over and pull each end to make a knot. Continue doing this until you have the length you want, usually 7–9 bags. Repeat this process two more times, so that you have three long rope strands. Braid the three strands. Finish the ends with duct tape; this will form your handles. Seven bags are just enough for a person 5 feet tall; a 5-feet, 9-inches youth would need nine bags. Seven bags measure out approximately 7½ feet long and this is just right for 5-feet height. You may want to make three examples using varying number of bags for participants to try out before making their own. This will give participants a visual on what the final product should look like and a range for the varying heights you will have in your group.

Caveat: Length will be determined based on the tension when braiding and size of each bag used. A tight braid will make a longer strand, and conversely, a loose braid will result in a shorter rope.

Project: HULA HOOP

Description: Hula hoops are basic exercise circles made of plastic tubing.

Community Partners: Schools/physical education teachers, community daycare, and summer programs may need exercise equipment.

Materials Needed: ¾-inch HDPE plastic irrigation tubing (sold in home improvement stores, usually a 10-foot minimum), coupler, pipe cutter or small saw, duct tape or decorative tape. Optional: Rice or beans to add to the tubing prior to sealing it up. This makes interesting sounds while the child uses the hoop.

Instructions: Tubing should be cut to 38 or 40–45 inches, but size is a preference. Insert coupler on one side of the tubing, and then insert the other side of tubing to connect and form a closed circle. Insert beans or rice, if desired, prior to forming the circle. Tape the tubing at the coupling.

8

Government and Community-Related Service Projects

*Never worry about numbers. Help one person at a time
and always start with the person nearest you.*
—Mother Teresa

We all live in a community. And as much as this book shows us how to make a difference in the world, our world starts at home in our communities and neighborhoods, whether located in cities, suburbs, on farms, ranches, or military bases. The projects in this chapter focus on community improvement and support for our military service personnel. Projects benefiting community-based organizations focused on animal welfare or health and wellness can be found in their respective chapters in this section.

Communication is the best way to find out what *your* community needs. Call the firehouse, ambulance corps, health-care facility, school or public library in your neighborhood and talk to their staff. Communication is the key to providing targeted help for a more significant impact in your community.

CALENDAR

Here are a few specific related events and celebrations to plan your programming:

Earth Day (April)
Veterans Day (November)
Military Family Appreciation Month (November)
Memorial Day (May)
Military Appreciation Month (May)
Senior Citizens Day (August 21)

COMMUNITY PROJECTS

Project: CARE PACKAGES FOR FIRST RESPONDERS
Description: A nice way to say thank-you is to create a care package for your local first responders. First responders such as firefighters, emergency medical technicians (EMTs), and police officers come to our aid every day. Fill care packages with sweets and treats, and

care items such as pain reliever, lip balm, and tissue. Include activity books, even though there's probably little down time for these heroic dedicated men and women. Make it a community event by involving local businesses.

Materials Needed: Have youth organize a collection drive for basket items. Ask local retailers for donations or gift cards for their establishment. They're part of the community, too, and surely would like to thank the local police or fire departments. Acquire a container to package the items and wrap them with clear plastic cellophane wrap. The container can be an upcycled wicker basket or shoebox decorated with cut-up magazine images or hand-drawn pictures.

Instructions: Fill the decorative container with the items and wrap. Have your group make personalized items to be included. Thank-you cards are a must! Also, make magnets with upbeat sayings and words of gratitude. If you have a button maker, adhesive magnetic tape affixed to the back will create these magnetic messages. The basket can be decorated with newspaper flowers or other DIY crafts. If possible, have youth drop off baskets to local first responders or invite first responders to your library for a day of gratitude. The inclusion of businesses, community members, and first responders develops connections and strengthens community ties.

Doing More: Our municipal service departments are filled with truly heroic men and women serving our communities near and far. Occasionally it is a sad day when a service member is lost in the line of duty. Florida teen Meghan O'Grady creates teddy bears made from the uniforms of the fallen. Blue Line Bears is a nonprofit started by this 14-year-old girl as a way to honor the fallen by providing their family members with keepsake bears created from their loved one's uniform. Each handmade bear comes with a personalized badge noting the police officer's name and badge number (Medel 2017). It is inspiring to see our youth stepping up and spreading compassion whether individually or as part of a group.

Create a rock garden filled with youth creations. Photo credit: Mindy Lawrence

Project: THE KINDNESS ROCK PROJECT (http:// thekindnessrocksproject.com/)

Description: Hand-painted rocks with encouraging messages left around the community as a random act of kindness.

Materials Needed: Acrylic paint and paint brushes, Sharpies; paint markers are an option that requires less cleanup, clear acrylic spray paint or Mod Podge, flat rocks or shells.

Instructions: Collect rocks, preferably flat ones. Shells can be used as an alternative if plentiful in your area. If neither is readily available, ask a local garden center for a donation of river rocks. Rocks should be clean and free of debris. Use Sharpies to trace out patterns, add details to images, or for writing upbeat sayings, if desired. Hashtag the rock with #TheKindnessRocksProject so recipients will be prompted to post their finds online to social media. Paint the rocks and allow time to dry. Spray the clear acrylic on the painted rock as a sealer and let dry. This is the preferred method. As an alternative for those who cannot use spray cans indoors, use Mod Podge as your sealer. Distribute the rocks among the community.

Modification: Walkway Rock Project or Art Installation
Have youth paint rocks to be added to your building's landscaping as either a walkway or an art installation, thereby adding to the beautification of the community.

Doing More: In the spring of 2017, a six-year-old girl, Ayel Morgenstern, learned that vandals destroyed tombstones in a Jewish cemetery in St. Louis. Tombstones were toppled and broken, and this compelled her to do something, to fight hate with kindness. She painted rocks with ladybugs and hearts and sent them to family members of those affected by the vandals (Pittman 2017). In Jewish tradition, it is customary to leave a stone behind on a tombstone when one visits a gravesite. Ayel's story demonstrates that not all maker projects need to be a partnership with an established organization and that we truly can be the catalyst for kindness, no matter our age.

Project: WELCOME NEW IMMIGRANT TO SCHOOL/COMMUNITY OR NEW KID WELCOME SURVIVAL KITS
Description: Create a welcome package of useful information such as phone numbers, map of school, area, school telephone contact numbers, office personnel, school calendar, list of sports, clubs and activities offered, town information such as the nearest hospital.
Community Partners: Schools and public libraries, translators, community service providers, service clubs.
Instructions: Gather pertinent information. Hand-decorate the folder to keep all papers within. Include some handmade items such as handmade bookmarks, welcome note, or buttons. Use your button maker to create magnets and buttons, as many teens like receiving buttons. These are two options to include if your group has access to the machine and supplies. Find someone to translate some of the items to match the linguistic need in your community. Schools typically hand a new student a planner with information, and other informational items are mailed home to parents. However, this project is a kid-to-kid exchange. Have a service club or National Honor Society members hand-deliver this welcome package face to face to the new students. It might be the needed welcome a new student needs and might develop into a lasting friendship or at least just a friendly face in the crowded hallway.

Project: LIBRARY BOOKMARKS
Description: This project was inspired by the Martin Library in York, Pennsylvania. As part of a youth library program the town's children created handmade bookmarks for visitors to take and use. These unique items were prominently placed on the circulation desk for all. Try this at your library. Your patrons will find it difficult to choose just one as each item is so unique. Your patrons will feel special taking one of

A variety of bookmarks.

these one-of-a-kind bookmarks. It is such a simple program and easy to implement with most ages.

Materials Needed: General supplies include cardstock paper in a variety of colors, stamps, stickers, colored pencils, upcycled magazines or wallpaper, origami paper—the possibilities are endless so use whatever you have on hand. For example, embroidery floss works well for a tassel, sparing yarn for other projects. However, if you have a large supply of yarn, use that. There's no right or wrong way to create. Use what you have. Single hole punch and yarn or ribbon if you wish to embellish the bookmark with a tassel. Beads can be added to the end of the tassel. It's up to your craft supply and the creativity of youth that will guide this project. Recipients of a handmade bookmark will be thrilled to have a pretty marker versus a store receipt or boarding pass to stick between pages. This is a simple way to do something special for the community. Here are several variations:

Button Bookmark

Materials: Wide ribbon, buttons, scissors, hot glue gun, and glue.

Instructions: Cut wide ribbon to approximately 12–14 inches long. Place ribbon between two buttons and hot glue together. Let dry for a few minutes.

Corner Bookmark

Materials: Upcycled envelopes, scissors, colored pencils, markers, and ink stamps or stickers.

Instructions: Cut corner edge off the envelope forming a triangle. For a nice touch, use decorative scissors with scalloped edges, if you have available. Now decorate with colored pencils, markers, and ink stamps or stickers.

Paint Chip Bookmark

Materials: Paint chip cards, single hole punch, yarn or ribbon for tassel.

Instructions: Go to the paint store and ask for discontinued paint chip cards. Using a hole punch, punch a hole at the top of the paint chip. Make a tassel out of yarn or ribbon and string through the hole.

Cereal Box Bookmark

Materials: Upcycled cereal and cookie boxes. Scissors, single hole punch, and ruler. Ribbon or yarn for tassel.

Instructions: Cut boxes into 2 × 7-inch strips. Using a hole punch, punch a hole at the top of the strip. Make a tassel out of yarn or ribbon and string through the hole.

Artwork Bookmark

Description: My husband is a watercolorist and not all his attempts are successful. As a way to recycle good quality watercolor paper and beautiful colors and designs, his discarded artwork is cut up into bookmarks. The strips are laminated to protect the image.

Materials: Scissors, single hole punch, ruler. Check with local art teachers or use artwork left from previous library programming.

Instructions: Cut up discarded artwork into 2 × 7-inch strips. Using a hole punch, punch a hole at the top of the strip. Make a tassel out of yarn or ribbon and string through the hole, if desired.

Jumbo Paperclip

Materials: Paperclips, preferably jumbo sized; yarn or ribbon; hot glue gun, glue, and decorative embellishment you have on hand.

Instructions: Create a tassel from ribbon or yarn or just tie a few pieces to the top end of a jumbo paperclip. You can embellish this further by hot gluing a bottle cap, button, or a small floral glass bead to the top end on top of the ribbons, if desired.

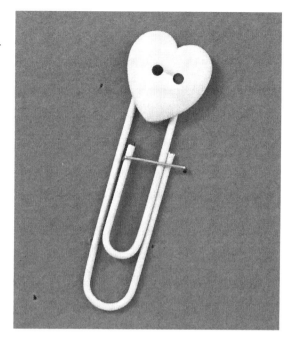

Nature Bookmark

Materials: Leaves or flowers; clear plastic book tape, scissors, single hole punch; yarn or ribbon.

Instructions: Using collected leaves or pressed flowers, sandwich nature items between clear plastic book tape. Trim to approximately 1 × 5 or 2 × 7 inches, depending on leaf sizing. Using a hole punch, punch a hole at the top of the strip. Make a tassel out of yarn or ribbon and string through the hole, if desired.

Book Spine Bookmark

Materials: Upcycled weeded books, X-Acto knife or scissor, matte gel medium, a brayer, single hole punch, cardstock.

Instructions: Upcycle weeded book by removing the spine using a scissor or X-Acto knife. Using matte gel medium, glue book spine onto heavy cardstock. Use a brayer (roller) to flatten the spine. Let dry. Using a hole punch, punch a hole at the top of the spine. Make a tassel out of yarn or ribbon and string through the hole, if desired. Eyelets will reinforce the hole, if you have this tool available.

3D Printed Bookmark

Materials: 3D printer, filament.

Instructions: Go to your favorite 3D maker community and download the file of your choice or create your own file design and print.

Project: LIBRARY BOOK KINDNESS NOTE

Description: In addition to bookmarks, youth may consider making a "kindness note" to be placed in random books in the library: handmade decorated notes recommending the book or just wishing the reader a happy day. This random act of kindness brightens the recipient's day.

Everyday cards or seasonal.

Materials Needed: Colorful construction paper or cardstock, scissors or die cut shapes to make notes interesting.

Instructions: Write and decorate notes.

Caveat: If notes include glued shapes, be sure the glue has dried prior to inserting it into a book. Also, make sure the note is not too thick to avoid damage the spine when inserted between pages.

Project: LIBRARY GREETING CARD SHOP

Description: Another way libraries can give back to community members is to create your own greeting card shop right in your library. Have your youth group create and decorate greeting cards for a variety of occasions: birthdays, get well, thanks, and so on. Place the cards in a clear plastic storage organizer with pockets, such as a shoe rack, and hang them up in a suitable location. Many organizers come with hooks or hangers; choose one that works well for your location. Alternatively, if you have a brochure rack collecting dust in the library basement, use that.

Community Partners: Use your library. For inclusive language cards, partner with schools or libraries with English as a new language programs or any social support group for new immigrants learning English.

Materials Needed: Card stock paper in various colors, colored markers or pencils, glue sticks, any "bling" you have available, such as rhinestones or gems. You can upcycle previously used cards by cutting off the tops or cutting out shaped designs and gluing them on your card stock. Use stickers, either new or ones you upcycled from mailing labels received for donations to charities. Just cut off the addresses and the pretty beach scene or cute animal is ready to be placed on your card. Decorative stamps or shaped die punches can add a creative, decorative touch. If you have a collection of these devices, use them and anything else at your disposal.

Instructions: Provide youth with the materials and ask them to be creative. It's that simple. When the session is finished, place the cards in the organizer, sorted by holiday, for community members to enjoy. Advertise this service to your patrons. Replenish as needed or desired. You can make this a year-long project by making and advertising current holiday card themes to your bank of everyday cards. And don't forget to be inclusive! Make cards in other languages based on your community's need. This is a great way to engage your limited English language proficient youth in library programming. Your English as a New Language school staff would make a good partner as would public libraries with a similar programming.

Project: LITERARY PAINTED CEILING TILES FOR LIBRARIES
Description: Painted ceiling tiles add beauty to a library facility.
Materials Needed: Ceiling tiles, acrylic paints, and paintbrushes
Instructions: Ask your youth group to paint literary book covers on the ceiling tiles to beautify their school or town library. You'll need to obtain ceiling tiles from custodial staff first. Set up a place to work and be sure to protect surfaces. Tiles will need to dry prior to installation.
Caveat: You need to obtain permission from the following persons: the school principal or library supervisor, the building and grounds supervisor of the facility, and your town fire marshal. There may be laws and fire codes that could prohibit this activity. Be sure to inquire first as each state and county may differ.

Project: POEMS FOR LOCAL RESTAURANTS
Description: To celebrate National Poetry Month (April), consider partnering up with a local restaurant to distribute free poems.
Community Partners: Local restaurants or businesses; any community venue that would like to spread the love of poetry and celebrate National Poetry Month.
Materials Needed: Plain lunch bag, colorful paper, scissors, ribbon, and markers or colored pencils.
Instructions: Select and print out poems on colorful paper (optional, white paper is fine, too.) The poems should be on the small size (4 × 5 inches) to fit in the paper lunch bags. Roll up the poem, and then tie the scroll with ribbon. Decorate the lunch bags with "Take One" or other sayings. Roll down the bags creating a bowl-like dispenser. Place poems in the bags and deliver to the venue, or arrange for pickup.
Caveats: Supervise the selection of poems to ensure they are a good fit for the venue. What works for a family restaurant might not be suited to date night restaurants. Poets.org allows you to filter results in themes category to poems in the public domain. Also, you'll need to do some asking around to find a willing partner to receive the poems. Prior communication is a must.

Project: COMMUNITY BOTTLE CAP MOSAIC
Community Partners: Mosaics can be made for community centers, agencies, libraries, or nursing homes to beautify their lobbies and other rooms in their facilities.
Materials Needed: Variety of upcycled plastic bottle caps, tacky glue, foam poster board in size desired.
Instructions: Start by organizing a bottle cap collection. Ask for donations of clean bottle caps of any size or color. Ask youth to come up with a design or provide one for them, particularly if you have a request, such as the initials of an agency. Mosaics can be replicas of famous artwork or written words. Trace out the design on the foam board. Gather the bottle caps and lay out on the board prior to gluing. Once you've got the design the way you want, start gluing. Allow time to dry.

Modifications: Can use foam board or even wood. When using wood, you can drill and screw the bottle caps to the board for a more permanent fixture.

Project: STICKTOGETHER (https://www.letsticktogether.com/)
Description: This is a community-building activity; the focus is on getting everyone to work together.
Materials Needed: StickTogether kit (most kits range from $30–$50). Custom images can be ordered ranging from $150–$275, depending on size. The kits come with a coded poster grid of a pixelated image, color stickers, and instructions. Every sticker counts so all participants matter, and since each square is labeled with a letter that corresponds to a color this activity is easy to implement for inclusive programming. Participants with limited English language proficiency will have no trouble participating.
Modification: Project Sticky Note Mosaic.
Materials Needed: Sticky notes, such as the Post-it brand or a generic brand, in various colors associated with your design, a pixelated design.
Instructions: Using an online pixel generator or book such as *Pixel Crochet* by Hannah Meur choose or develop a design. 3M Post-it has several easy-to-follow suggestions for creating your own pixel art: http://www.post-it.com/3M/en_US/post-it/ideas/articles/7-tips-for-creating-post-it-super-sticky-note-pixel-art/. Have youth work in groups as a team-building exercise.

GARDENING PROJECTS

Project: SEED BOMBS
Description: Beautify your community while attracting birds, butterflies, and bees. This project helps the environment by providing flowers for pollinators and makes your community a more beautiful place.
Community Partners: Local cooperative extension, community garden club, school environmental group or garden club.
Materials Needed: Native seeds (plants that are hardy and non-invasive to your locale), clay, compost or potting mix, water. Be sure to check if your local cooperative extension offers free seeds.
General Recipe: 5 parts clay, 1 part compost (potting soil), 1 part seeds. You'll need measuring cups, spoons, and something to serve as a mixing bowl. Disposable aluminum baking pans or dollar store plastic buckets are easy to rinse off and use multiple times for this and other projects.
Instructions: Work in an area that you don't mind dirt! This can be a bit messy, so put down some newspapers or other protective items on your workspace, and possibly floor. Mix clay and compost together. Clay will be hard but will loosen up a bit from the warmth of your hands. If it's still too hard to mix, add a little bit of water a few drops at a time. You do not want a soupy mix. Your mixture should feel gritty and dough-like. Gradually add seeds, kneading them into the dough-like mixture. Break off pieces and roll into a 3–4-inch ball.
Caveat: Choose seeds native to your area only; you don't want to cause environmental damage by introducing an invasive plant species, nor do you want to go through the time and expense of creating seed bombs for plants not hardy enough to survive your climate or local conditions. If you are unsure, contact a local cooperative extension for professional advice.

Project: MASON BEE HOUSE

Description: Help create a healthy and beautiful environment by encouraging mason bees to live in your community. Mason bees are great pollinators, but they don't make their own houses like other bees; they look for openings and use what's available. Help these essential pollinators find a home in your community.

Community Partners: In schools, your garden club, or 4-H. You'll need to hang the houses outdoors when completed. So, either participants take these home to hang or you'll need to find willing recipients for the bee houses. This arrangement with a willing community partner allows youth living in apartments or shelters to participate in the program.

Materials Needed: Upcycled metal can (soup cans are good but any can size will suffice including tomato sauce or coffee cans), hollow reeds usually found in garden centers (bamboo stalks and rolled up scrap paper are alternatives), twine, a small pruning saw to cut the reeds, and hammer and nail. Optional: Yellow spray paint. Money Saver: If a community member has bamboo growing in his or her yard, you can ask if he or she is willing to prune some stalks for this project. This will make the project practically free.

Instructions: Clean the can. Remove one end of the can with a safety edge can opener so there are no sharp edges. Using a nail and a hammer, make a hole at the bottom of the can so that you can thread twine through it for hanging. Paint the can a bright color, if desired. Bright colors attract bees. While can is drying, cut the reeds to the length of the can. Insert the twine through the hole at the bottom and out the front. Tie a knot for hanging. Now, insert the reeds in the can filling it completely. Pack the reeds tightly.

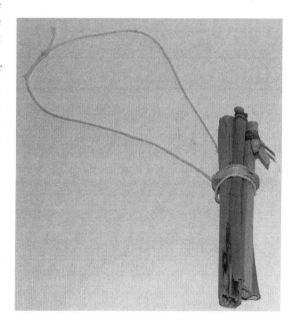

Caveats: Use a safety can opener, known as safe-cut, smooth-edge, or safe-edge, so that participants don't get cut on sharp edges when handling the cans. If participants notice birds pecking at their bee house, instruct them to cover it with chicken wire. This should keep the birds at bay.

Modification: If you don't want to collect cans, just tie up a dozen 6-inch reeds with twine and place in a good location.

A simple bee house.

Project: COMMUNITY GARDEN PLANT MARKERS

Description: Many neighborhoods have a community gardens. Pitch in and create decorative plant markers for your community or school garden.

Community Partners: Local cooperative extensions, community garden groups, school garden club, your buildings, and grounds staff.

Materials Needed: Plant markers can be made from a wide range of materials from craft sticks to clay pot fragments. Ask a local physician for tongue depressors! Large rocks can be used, too. There are numerous possibilities; start with readily accessible supplies. Use a wood burner tool on any of the wood-based projects, if you have this tool in your collection. This specialized tool usually comes with decorative tips and some sets, a full alphabet for spelling out messages. All markers will withstand outdoor use better if a sealant is used after the item is labeled and decorated. Use a clear spray sealant or polyurethane. For indoor use, sealant is beneficial but optional.

Carefully peel back the bark.

Here are several variations:

Tile Marker
Materials: Upcycled ceramic tiles, Sharpie markers, sealant.
Instructions: Decorate donations of leftover tiles from home improvement jobs using Sharpie markers. Apply sealant and allow to dry.

Bottle Cork/Chopstick Marker
Materials: Corks, chopsticks, acrylic paints, Sharpie marker, hand drill, and 3/16-inch bit, sealant.
Money Saver: Purchase corks or collect upcycled wine bottle corks. Purchase chopsticks or ask for a donation from a local establishment. Corks and chopsticks are frequent junk draw finds. You should be able to acquire these items through donations making this a low-cost project.
Instructions: For colorful markers, paint the chopsticks in different colors using acrylic paints. Let dry. Using a hand drill and 3/16-inch bit, make a hole 1 inch deep in each cork. Decorate and label each cork using Sharpie markers. Push the chopstick onto the cork or gently tap with a hammer. A dab of wood glue is optional; the cork should be snug. If desired, apply sealant and allow it to dry.
Caveat: If you don't have access to a hand drill or don't want to use one with your youth, use kabob skewers instead. Push the pointy end through the cork. Chopsticks are sturdier, however.
Brick Marker
Materials: Bricks, acrylic paints, sealant.
Instructions: This is a heavy option. But free bricks can be collected from leftover home and landscaping projects. Decorate and label them with names of plants using acrylic paints. Let dry. Using a clear sealant spray, cover the brick and let dry 15–20 minutes.

Rock Marker

Instructions: Follow the instructions found in the Kindness Rock Project. Decorate and label clean rocks with the names of plants. Apply a sealant.

Branch Marker

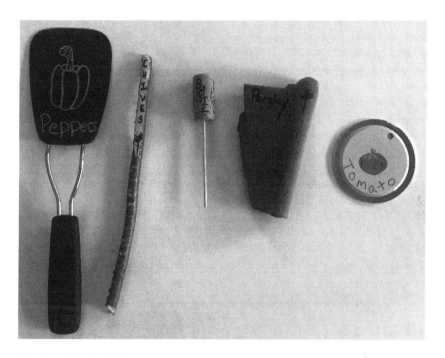

A variety of garden markers.

Materials: Branches, pruner, vegetable peeler or knife, Sharpie markers, sealant.

Instructions: Collect branches approximately ½-inch diameter; using pruners trim them to desired length about 6–10 inches. Using a vegetable peeler (or a knife), peel away several inches of bark. On the exposed wood, write the name of the plant using a Sharpie marker. Or if you have access to a wood burning tool, write the names of each plant. Apply sealant.

Caveat: This activity may dull the vegetable peeler. Determine if your youth can handle knives or prep the wood branches for youth prior to activity.

Wooden Spoon Marker

Materials: Upcycled spoons, Sharpie markers, sealant.

Instructions: Run a spoon collection drive and upcycle either wooden or plastic spoons. Using colorful Sharpie markers, decorate and label each spoon. Decorative images and messages can be added using a wood burning tool. Apply sealant for outdoor use.

Clothespin/Craft Stick Marker

Materials: Craft sticks, clothespins, Sharpie markers or wood burning tool, if desired, sealant.

Instructions: Using markers, decorate and label the wood portion of the craft stick and the clothespin. This can be done with Sharpie markers or a wood-burning tool. Attach the clothespin at a right angle at the top of the craft stick. Apply sealant if for outdoor use.

Money Saver: Ask health-care professionals for a donation of tongue depressors. Dowels or chopsticks can be used, too. Clothespins can be found in your local dollar store.

NURSING HOME AND ASSISTED-CARE FACILITIES

Project: NURSING HOME ART GALLERY

Description: Have youth create a collection of artwork to be displayed at a local nursing home. The elderly in the community will enjoy the display of art brought to them.

Community Partners: Contact your local nursing home or rehabilitation facility to inquire if they are willing to provide space for your group's work and if there are any special requirements such as size of artwork. You may offer the work to display for a set period of time, or it may be a donation to brighten the residents' rooms. Art teachers can provide technical assistance, if needed.

Materials Needed: Canvas, paints, mixed media, brushes; hanging hardware—frame hanging wire and picture frame ring hanger.

Instructions: Allow youth to be creative in their designs, provided the images are friendly and upbeat. Serene images are fine, but dark or disturbing depictions may not be welcome as they may put the residents at ill ease. Allow time to dry. Make sure paintings are ready to hang with framing hardware attached to back of artwork.

Caveat: Assistance will be needed for driving over the cache of work and hanging the items. The facility may have custodial staff available for this, so inquire.

Modification: Project Color a Smile (http://colorasmile.org/)

Description: If there are no nursing homes or assisted living facilities in your area or you prefer to implement a smaller art project, consider participating in Color a Smile. This group collects drawings and distributes them to senior citizens, troops overseas, and anyone in need of a smile. This is a good way to recycle drawings, too. Just place drawings in an envelope and mail to Color a Smile offices and they will distribute them to those who need. Your group can participate with this organization or form your own life line for nursing homes or seniors in your neighborhood or for local heroes serving in the military. Have group members collect names of community members who could benefit from a smile and get to it!

Dolls are stuffed though the opening in the leg.

Start with the head, then arms, then chest, and the legs.

The dolls should be firm, but not hard.

If the legs or arms flop, more stuffing is needed.

Use a chopstick to push in stuffing.

Sew the opening closed in the leg with needle and thread.

Stuffing hole ⇨

Use a simple bear template.

Project: BEAR-Y NEEDED COMFORT

Description: Police officers often find themselves with a frightened child due to a variety of unfortunate circumstances. These children need comfort in these unpleasant situations.

Community Partner: Police departments. September 9 is National Teddy Bear Day.

Materials Needed: Assorted fabric, Poly-Fil stuffing, needle and thread or sewing machine, simple one-piece bear pattern template, chopsticks.

Instructions: Create a bear template to make a bear approximately 6–7 inches tall. Cut out pattern on fabric creating two pieces. Place the fabric pieces right side facing each other and sew together leaving a 2-inch opening. Turn out the fabric right side out. Stuff it with Poly-Fil. You may need help pushing the stuffing in the arms and legs; use a chopstick or similar shaped item, if needed. Sew the opening closed. Deliver bears to police station.

Caveat: You can add button eyes and yarn hair, but it's probably best to leave the bear plain as embellishments may pose a choking hazard for young children and children with an oral fixation.

Project: COMMUNITY SCARVES

Description: Knit or crochet scarves and leave around town with a note "If needed . . ." or "I'm not lost. . . ." Participants may research community agencies (soup kitchens, shelters) and include this information with phone numbers on the "If needed" label.

Community Partners: Soup kitchens, pantries, shelters, public library. Knitting and crochet groups to serve as mentors or join in with teens.

Materials Needed: Yarn, crochet hooks or knitting needles, paper for labels, preferably cardstock, hole punch and yarn scraps to attach labels. Or, use a safety pin to attach labels.

Instructions: Knit or crochet scarves using your favorite pattern depending on the abilities of your participants. Print or write out "If needed" labels. Hole punch the label, and then attach it using yarn scraps or a safety pin. Leave scarves outside the library or around town where those who need them will find the scarves.

Project: NO-SEW SCARVES

Community Partners: Homeless shelters or any group working to clothe the community.

Materials Needed: Fleece, scissors, ruler or measuring tape. Optional: Tape, beads.

Instructions: Cut fleece into a strip of approximately 9 inches wide by 5 feet long: longer or shorter as per your preference. Measure 4 inches from the bottom of the strip. To mark this off you may put tape across the strip or use chalk to make a line. Cut this area into ½-inch strips. Tie each strip into a knot at the top. You are done unless you want to add beads. If so, string beads through the knotted strip and knot at the bottom to hold beads in place.

INCLUSIVE COMMUNITY EASTER EGG HUNT

The following projects allow for an inclusive community event, providing children with visual and mobile disabilities the opportunity to participate independently. Collaborate with town officials, faith-based groups, and disability organizations in your community.

Project: MAGNETIC EASTER EGGS

Description: Physically disabled children with mobility issues have a hard time participating in community events without modifications. Unable to reach the eggs on the ground, these children remain on the sidelines while their peers gather eggs. Children in wheelchairs can independently gather eggs using a long magnetic stick to pick up magnetic eggs. We should strive for inclusive community events.

Materials Needed: Small plastic Easter eggs, magnets, preferably ceramic magnets as they are stronger, long craft stick or yard stick, superglue.

Instructions: Affix magnets inside or outside the plastic egg using superglue. Glue a magnet to the end of a long stick. Allow glue to dry.

Caveat: Magnets should not be ingested. Small magnets pose a choking hazard and other damages if swallowed. Very young children and those with an oral fixation should be supervised.

Project: BEEPING EGGS

Description: Blind and visually impaired children cannot fully participate in community Easter Egg Hunt events. Parents or guardians have to lead the child to the egg and place their hand upon the item for collection and placement in their basket. Making audible eggs allows the child to independently find an egg using sound instead of sight.

Materials Needed: Large plastic eggs, toggle switch, a piezo beeper, a 9-volt battery, a battery clip, drill, solder iron, and electrical tape.

Instructions: Use instructions provided by David Hyche at https://www.iabti.org/media/pdf/InstructionsforBeepingEgg.pdf.

Caveat: This activity requires a drill and soldering. We allow both tools in our library, under supervision. If you're not comfortable with these tools or they're not allowed in your facility, this is not the project for you.

Project: DIGITAL ARCHIVE PROJECT—LOCAL HISTORY PRESERVED

Description: Preserve your school yearbooks or local history by digitizing your treasures! Instead of sitting in archival boxes wrapped in archival tissue never seeing the light of day, save school and library records from obscurity. Preserve local history for future generations.

Community Partners: Seek out a local graduate library school with an archival program for added assistance; any organization that wants to preserve documents such as local historical societies.

Materials Needed: A scanner and digital storage space cloud, hard drive, or jump drive, or a combination of two for backup. Access to the items to be preserved.

Instructions: Working with students, provide instruction on how to handle delicate documents. Have youth scan one page at a time and label each section according to a template you agree upon. For example: Four-digit year_Title of Document_Page#. It doesn't matter the arrangement of the file information, so long as it's consistent. This is to ensure uniformity from volume to volume and item to item, reducing confusion down the road. Decide where you want the information to "live" such as the local historical society, school website, or some other platform and obtain necessary permission. Copyright should not apply, but you should consult with historians or archivists in your area if you have any concerns. If you don't have a scanner or you want several youth scanning documents simultaneously, several phone apps are available, including Google Drive. If your library has iPads you can load the scanning apps needed and get the job done quicker!

Caveat: Archival procedure should be adhered to for important items. That is to say, white cotton gloves should be worn if necessary and no ink pens should be near the items potentially causing markups. Fragile and important documents should be handled by staff only.

LITTLE FREE LIBRARY

On Staten Island, New York, HEALTH for Youth, a nonprofit organization working with young people to reach their full potential, partnered with the New York Police Department (NYPD) to provide a unique situation for community members. The 120th Precinct of the NYPD now has a Little Free Library in the precinct's lobby so if children happen to find themselves at the station for whatever reason, they have access to free books (*NY1News*, 2016). This is a beautiful community partnership. The folks at Little Free Library have formed the Kids, Community and Cops Program to help increase youth literacy and family engagement and forge community partnerships, and police departments across the country are participating. The HEALTH for Youth group collaborated with the Staten Island Makerspace to create another Little Free Library on Staten Island (Gonzalez 2015). These are some great examples of potential community partners.

Project: LITTLE FREE LIBRARY OR COMMUNITY BOOK EXCHANGE
Description: The Little Free Library (https://littlefreelibrary.org/) is a trademarked name, and if using this moniker, you must register with Little Free Library. Library kits that can be put together in a few hours with the step-by-step instructions provided are sold on its website. Or, your group can build their own library out of recycled and reclaimed materials. Remember if you call it a Little Free Library you must register and pay a fee of around $50; if not registered call it a community book exchange or street library. Little Free Library accepts purchase orders, making it easier for schools and libraries to place an order. It's not enough to create the library case. The library needs to be placed in an approved accessible location. This is where young people can learn a lot about community government. With the assistance of an adult mentor, youth will need to investigate potential locations and then inquire at local government offices as to the regulations regarding this activity. This could be a zoning administrator who can shed light on city or town zoning ordinances that affect the location or even the ability to initiate this project. There may be government fees involved. Do not start the project until it is determined permission is granted, fees paid, and permits acquired. A Little Free Library can be placed anywhere you have permission to do so, be it a school, local business, town facility, or private property.
Community Partners: Young Politicians Club, Chamber of Commerce Club, Student Government, and Book Club are some of your groups in a school setting. In the community, be sure to seek out local business owners and government officials.
Doing More: In 2017, The Little Free Library launched an Action Book Club, part traditional book group where members read books and have discussions and part service club in that group members come together not only to read and discuss books but to also participate in group service projects to benefit their community. Sign-up is free, and many book recommendations and service ideas can be found on its website. Form a group, read a book, take positive action in your neighborhood, and share your story on the Little Free Library website. That simple. The Action Book Club's 2018 theme is Everyday Heroes, which celebrates acts of bravery, character, and kindness that transform our world in ways big and small. There are other book clubs combining reading and activism; find one that fits your group or form your own!
Modification: A recent twist on the community book exchange is a "blessings box" or "yard-based food pantries." Styled like a Little Free Library, the purpose of this community box is to exchange and provide food and personal care items. See Project: Little Free Pantry/Food Exchange Box for more information.

Project: GAMES FOR CHANGE (G4C) STUDENT CHALLENGE

Description: This is a "digital game design competition that invites students to create games about issues impacting their communities" and a great way to engage your techie youth with potential to win prizes and receive recognition for their creations.

Caveat: Right now, only middle and high school students in New York City, North Texas, or Pittsburgh-area public school districts are eligible to participate. Check out Game for Change's website (http://www.gamesforchange.org/) for games to play with your group and for inspiration to create your own digital games. On the site you'll find other game design competitions and information about upcoming events and gatherings.

Community Partners: You may want to pair up with a computer science teacher to act as a mentor.

Materials Needed: Games youth create need to be playable in either a free or open platform (i.e., Scratch, Gamestar Mechanic, Unity, Game Salad). Your group will need access to computers, the Internet, and one of the programs listed above downloaded to either their device or library computers.

Instructions: Go to the website for up-to-date specific rules, eligibility, and submission dates. Games must be about one of the three Challenge Themes (Climate Change, Future Communities, or Local Stories and Immigrant Voices). Games may be submitted individually or as a team.

MILITARY

Not sure how to help our service men and women? Call your local VA hospital or

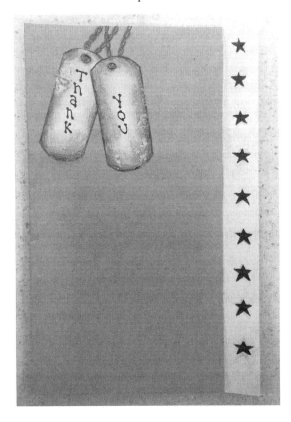

USO and ascertain their needs. Working locally is always the best starting point for implementing service projects. However, be aware there are overseas healthcare system counterparts for service personnel. Landstuhl Hospital located in Germany is the largest overseas military hospital and runs the Landstuhl Hospital Care Project, benefiting service members hospitalized outside the United States. Be sure to check its website (http://www.landstuhlhospitalcare project.org/) for current needs. In the ever-changing world in which we live, checking current needs is always a must.

Arts-Based Projects
Project: CARDS FOR SOLDIERS OR VETERANS
Materials Needed: Cardstock paper in a variety of colors (recommended

20 lb or higher), colored pencils, crayons and markers in a variety of colors. Optional: Stickers, picture cutouts, and glue.

Community Partners: Many organizations collect these cards. Do a Google search of your area or ask a local recruiting office, VFW, or other veterans association to help you find a local group. Red Cross Annual Holiday Mail for Heroes campaign is now called Holidays for Heroes. To participate, contact your local Red Cross office. For a personal touch some of your cards can be sent to recent graduates of your school or to family members of your staff. Military will not release names and personal information, but chances are someone in your building or organization has a family member serving and would be happy to provide you with an address. Youth really like to address a note to someone specific and even more, love hearing where that person is stationed and what they're doing. If you can get a photo(s) of the local service member(s), add it to your supply table; it will generate lots of interest and motivation. It's up to you to send these cards to strangers or to community members.

Instructions: Fold cardstock in half. Decorate. Write a note. Give to partner agency. Here are some basic guidelines:

- Address your cards to "service member."
- Write a positive upbeat note!
- No glitter, sparkles, or sequins. No scents.
- Do not enclose any items with your cards.
- Include your name and generic information about where you're from, but do not include additional personal information such as e-mail, phone number, or address.
- Do not date notes as they may be sent out at different times of the year.
- Don't include envelopes.

Project: BLANK CARDS FOR SOLDIERS

Instructions: Follow the instructions above but leave the inside of the card blank. Blank cards are given to service personnel for their use. Sometimes, soldiers can't access a greeting card store due to hospitalization or deployment to a war zone. In these cases, soldiers can use your creative blank cards to send home to their loved ones, wishing their mom a happy birthday or congratulations on a cousin's new baby. Birthdays, anniversaries, and babies continue to arrive regardless of deployment. Blank cards give soldiers an opportunity to be part of a special occasion.

Photos of military personnel will add a personal touch to this project.

Community Partners: Contact USO, recruiting offices, military bases in your area. Sometimes all you need is a coworker with a deployed family member who is happy to receive free items.

Doing More: Additionally, while you're honoring to our men and women in service, let's not forget about our canine heroes! Military working doges are a vital part of the armed forces. Care packages for the dogs and handlers can be sent to a variety of organizations such as the United States War Dog Association (http://www.uswardogs.org/). As always, be sure to check directly with each organization as to what it needs and is willing to accept. Communication is key!

Project: RED POPPIES FOR VETERANS DAY (November 11)

Description: Why do this project? To remember our soldiers who fought in World War I. To give one's life in service to country should never be forgotten. Using the poem *In Flanders Fields*, written by John McCrae (1872–1918), will have youth learning about a most bloody battle in Flanders Field (Belgium) during World War I and remembering those soldiers whose lives were cut short in service to their country. As a nation and a society, it is up to every generation to keep the memory of the fallen alive. Traditionally, small poppies are distributed by the American Legion, but youth can make their own as well. Also, larger poppies using the plate project can be hung on classroom doors or around town as a community celebration of remembrance.

Materials Needed: Red crepe paper and black crepe paper; use party streamer rolls; red cupcake holders, black button, black or green pipe cleaner, paper plates, glue, and scissors.

Instructions:

Small poppies: Materials—Red paper cupcake holders, black crepe paper, or a black button, glue, and scissors, black or green pipe cleaner. Stack 3–4 cupcake holders. Push the pipe cleaner through the middle of the holder and back out. Twist the pipe cleaner to close. Ruffle the cupcake wrapper to give it a more flower-like appearance. Glue black button or black paper to the center of the poppy.

Paper plate poppies: Apply glue to a paper plate. Working in a circular motion going from outside in, line the plate with red crepe paper. Try to ruffle the crepe paper instead of lying flat; this will give a more realistic flower-like appearance. Cover the plate completely. Make a loose crumpled ball out of the black crepe paper. In the center of the plate (flower) glue the black crepe paper ball.

Modifications: Poppies can be crocheted or even 3D printed! Choose the right format for your group!

In Flanders fields the poppies blow
Between the crosses, row on row,
That mark our place, and in the sky,
The larks, still bravely singing, fly,
Scarce heard amid the guns below.

We are the dead; short days ago
We lived, felt dawn, saw sunset glow,
Loved and were loved, and now we lie
In Flanders fields.

Take up our quarrel with the foe!
To you from failing hands we throw
The torch; be yours to hold it high!
If ye break faith with us who die
We shall not sleep, though poppies grow
In Flanders fields.
         —John McCrae, May 3, 1915

Doing More: Set up a Missing Man Table as part of your library display during Veteran's Day or Memorial Day. Ask community members for a loan of World War II memorabilia to round out your display and to make the experience more educational. The Missing Man Table honors service members who have fallen, went missing, or held captive. Each item on the table represents a specific struggle or sacrifice. Read *America's White Table* by Margot Theis Raven to your group for an explanation of the symbolism of each item. Partner with your local Boy Scout troop; they may be willing to set the display up for you.

Project: PARACORD SURVIVAL BRACELET
Description: Lifesaving cord available to military personnel quickly needed.
Materials Needed: 550 paracord, scissors, instructions available on Operation Gratitude website where you can find videos, including left-handed instructions! They also sell pre-cut and sealed bracelet kits if you prefer. Fill out donation form if making these items for Operation Gratitude.
Instructions: Access Operation Gratitude kits and directions at https://opgrat.wordpress.com/2014/04/23/paracord-survival-bracelets-faqs-tips/.
Caveats: Only neutral colors! Soldiers do their best to blend in their environment. Snipers can spot bright colors from quite a distance! Remember these bracelets are designed to help in an emergency, not cause one. Depending on the ages you're working with, this could be a frank discussion on the service and sacrifice men and women of the armed forces perform for us. You know your group, so decide accordingly.

Knitting and Crocheting for Military Causes

The Caron yarn company partnered with the Children of Fallen Patriots Foundation to support Gold Star families in all branches of the military. The foundation provides college scholarships and educational counseling for military children who have lost a parent in the line of duty. When you purchase the Caron United line of yarn, a portion of the proceeds benefits the Foundation. In 2014, Caron United launched a "Make the World's Biggest Stocking" event hoping to get listed in the Guinness Record books. Volunteers knitted or crocheted 3 feet by 3 feet blankets, which were then stitched together to create a giant stocking. After the stocking was completed and displayed, it was then disassembled and the blankets cleaned and donated to military charities. Making this is a fun and unusual way to contribute.

Caron received the Guinness World Record title for the largest knit/crochet stocking at 1,600 lb and 139 feet tall and 74 feet wide. The company put out a call for help on Veterans Day 2014, and over 1,100 contributors donated blankets benefiting military hospitals. According to the company this was a onetime event, and it does not plan to repeat the drive. However, it does bring to light the numerous possibilities that will not be found in this book. It's always best to follow community groups, crafting groups, and acts

of kindness groups on social media and make others aware of the types of projects you're looking for so that they can pass the information along to your group. There are so many organizations and individuals looking for help, and we just need to make the right connections.

Project: AMPUTEE STUMP COVERS
Description/Caveat: As discussed previously, you know your youth. The nature of war can be graphic and traumatic, as in the loss of a limb. Decide how candid you want to be when discussing the project among your group. Stump covers can be made for any limbless person, due to a variety of medical conditions, including diabetes. You could implement this project during American Diabetes Month (November). Again, youth may ask questions—decide how much detail you wish to share or choose another knitting project instead.

Community Partners: Your local VA Hospital, VFW groups, hospitals, and diabetic support groups.
Materials Needed: Yarn, knitting needles, patterns from http://www.knotsoflove.org/patterns.
Instructions: Follow instructions on the Knots of Love pattern.

Project: KNITTED OR CROCHETED HATS AND SCARVES
Description/Community Partner: Operation Gratitude (http://www.operationgratitude.com/). Handmade with Love program donates handmade hats and scarves to men and women deployed overseas. They are added to care packages the group sends. Hats are great for your first responders in your community as well!
Materials Needed: Yarn, crochet hook or knitting needles, scissors.
Instructions: Free patterns can be found here: https://www.operationgratitude.com/wp-content/uploads/2017/04/HandmadewithLovePatterns_2017.pdf. Or use one of your own. Mail to Operation Gratitude (address in Appendix C).

Project: WARMTH FOR WARRIORS—HATS AND HOLIDAY STOCKINGS
Description: Warmth for Warriors (http://warmthforwarriors.com/) provides your handmade hats to service men and women at home and overseas. In addition to hats, Warmth for Warriors collects handmade miniature holiday stockings that are distributed during the holiday season.

Materials Needed: Yarn, knitting needles or crochet hooks, scissors.

Instructions: Easy patterns can be found on the Warmth for Warriors website (http:// warmthforwarriors.com/knit.html). Printable PDF files are easy to distribute to your group. These are basic patterns for a skull cap-type hat and for a miniature stocking; use theirs or your own similar favorite patterns. Pack up your donations, noting what type of yarn used, and ship to Warmth for Warriors.

Caveat: Any type of yarn can be used: wool, acrylic, etc. However, only 100 percent wool yarn hats are sent overseas.

Sewing Projects

Project: COOL-TIES POLYMER NECK BANDS

Description: It's hot over there! Many service members are deployed in areas where temperatures reach triple digits Fahrenheit. Neck bands are an easy way to reduce body temperature and provide relief from the heat. Water-absorbing polymer granules are used.

Community Partner: Operation Gratitude.

Materials Needed: 2 teaspoons of Cool-Tie polymer (approximately $20 for 2 lb at watersorb.com), 4-inch strip of fabric 45 inches long, scissors, thread, sewing machine, tape measure.

Instructions: Can be found at WaterSorb (https://watersorb.com/ pages/cool-ties) and at Operation Gratitude (https://www.operation gratitude.com/wishlist/). You are basically sewing fabric into a tube shape and filling it with the polymer. Sew shut the ends of tube.

Neck band and polymer granules.

Caveats: Operation Gratitude requests the following: choose subtle colors, Cool Ties should be made with 100 percent cotton, no fringe.

Modification: Project Helmet Cooler (Polymer Fill). Make 7-inch fabric rounds filled with polymer granules.

Doing More: Looking for a personalized touch? Identify local military families and inquire as to their needs and how your group can help. Not all your projects need to be donated to an organization. No doubt there are military families in your community. Help them out! May is Military Family Appreciation Month. Below are a few more ideas.

Project: PERSONALIZED QUILTS AND PILLOWS

Description: Operation Kid Comfort for the children of deployed parents provides comfort from the stress of separated families. Organized through the Armed Services YMCA on various military bases, a personalized pillow or quilt can be requested. Requestor sends photographs of deployed parent with family images and volunteers will make the items, either a pillow or a blanket. Regardless of where you live, you can volunteer to finish quilts for Operation Kid Comfort. Call the Armed Services YMCA national office for more information (800–597–1260). Fort Drum, New York, alone has supplied more than 3,000 families with quilts. Established groups at Armed Services YMCAs across the United States, including Hawaii and Alaska, and overseas in Germany facilitate this service (Bell 2009).

Community Partners: You may wish to consult with a sewing teacher and technology mentors if you have any concerns about this project and whether it is right for your kids. Also, you may want to send items to local military families or overseas to their deployed loved one.

Materials Needed: Fabric, computer printer fabric sheets, sewing machine, thread and scissors; access to a printer and digital photos.

Instructions: Follow the directions on the fabric sheet container. Print out your digital image(s) on the sheets. Sew fabric sheet into your project, whether quilt or pillow, using the manufacturer's directions. You'll need youth with digital skills manipulating images and some with sewing skills. These tasks can be split between youth with those respective strengths.

Caveat: Fabric sheets can be used with either inkjet or laser printers. Some brands can use either printer. Be sure to purchase the appropriate brand as per your equipment available as misuse may damage your printer. Also, some brands are washable and others are dry clean only. Read the product description carefully prior to purchase.

Modification: The pillow project can be made for families when your group participates in adopting a family through Habitat for Humanity. The volunteer coordinator at your local Habitat for Humanity office will assign a family to your group and can provide you with family photos for use in this personalized project.

Project: PILLOWCASES FOR TROOPS

Description: Join Cindy's Baking Angels (http://cindysbakingangels.net/) in this ongoing project sending homemade pillowcases to deployed troops. This organization is a good one to follow as each month a unit is adopted and specific items are made for service members from cooling neckties to knitted hats. There's even a referral page; you might want to encourage your group to refer a local hero!

Community Partners: Cindy's Baking Angels, local military agencies.

Materials Needed: Fabric, sewing machine, needle, thread, scissors.

Instructions: Use a favorite template for a standard pillowcase size; there are several listed in this book, too. On Cindy's website there are video tutorials and instructions: http://cindysbakingangels.net/Pillowcases.html. Sew and ship to Cindy's Baking Angels.

Modification: For a no-sew option, decorate pillowcases using plain premade store-bought cases and either fabric markers or fabric paint. Check your local military-related agencies to see if this version is acceptable for donation. Not all agencies or organizations will accept this version.

Project: MILITARY MEMORIAL BEARS

Description: One of the most compassionate service projects that can be performed for families of fallen service members is the sewing of memorial bears. These handmade bears provide family members with comfort during the mourning process. The Matthew

Freeman Project (http://freemanproject.org/) honors the life and service to country of Captain Matthew Freeman, a marine killed in action in Afghanistan. Fallen service members' families may request a bear be made from the uniform of the fallen. This organization will put family members in touch with a willing seamstress to complete the bears requested. If you have skilled sewers in your group, this may be an activity you can recommend. Qualified sewers can contact the folks at the Matthew Freeman Project to sign on and will be given specific instructions. Not all projects in this book need to be accomplished by a group; individuals play an important role in service. It is our job as youth leaders to direct and inspire not only youth groups but also individuals to their desired path toward expressing empathy.

9

Going Global

Do your little bit of good where you are;
it is those little bits of good put all together that overwhelm the world.
—Desmond Tutu

Making a difference need not be limited to one state, country, or continent. Go global in your efforts to make a difference in someone's life. Look to the United Nations Sustainable Development Goals (SDGs): a global set of 17 goals to end poverty, protect the planet, and ensure prosperity for all. SDGs can be found on the United Nations website at www.un.org/sustainabledevelopment/sustainable-development-goals/. Educators can pair projects with SDGs for an added educational awareness.

Typically, it's best to raise funds for global relief as that's what international organizations need the most. However, there are some tangible projects your youth participants can create.

EDUCATION

Aptly stated by Nobel Prize laureate Malala Yousafzai, "Education is the best weapon we have to fight poverty, ignorance and terrorism." However, many children do not have access to schools, or have interrupted formal education. According to UNICEF, "1 in 4 of the world's school-aged children live in countries affected by crises" (2016, 90). Many children around the world have to cease school attendance for various reasons including conflict, poverty, and menstruation. Young girls are most affected as they are more likely than boys to drop out of school. The series of projects below directly affect access to education, especially for girls. Challenges stemming from the availability of clean water, clothing, and menstrual hygiene supplies affect the access to education for young girls globally. Girls are typically tasked with the daily chore of obtaining water for family needs, pulling them away from time spent on schooling. And not having access to new clothing or menstrual supplies causes an increased dropout rate disproportionately among girls versus boys. So many common items we take for granted each day (water, clothing, sanitary products) allow our children attend school. The last subsection of the category, Literacy and Cultural Diversity, emphasizes teaching our youth about the importance of education as seen through the challenges of youth globally through literacy.

Clean Water

Water is life. Every living thing needs water. H2O for Life (https://www.h2oforlife schools.org/) is an organization that pairs schools in the United States with schools abroad that need funds to provide clean water and sanitation. This is not a project in which an item is made and shipped to a partner school. However, it is an important topic and one that needs awareness. The H2O for Life organization could greatly benefit from one of your DIY craft sales! Your youth group can research and choose a school to support, raise funds, and raise awareness. As part of the activities, you can obtain a water purification kit and have your kids make dirty water potable. This is a fascinating and educational hands-on activity that raises awareness of access to potable water. While our children obtain water from a faucet at home or school, youth in developing nations have to retrieve water from wells and rivers miles away. This job often falls to young girls, diminishing their time from school and studies (Byker 2017). While this is a matter of water insecurity, it directly affects access to education particularly for girls. Additionally, access to clean water and sanitation affects not only schooling but also health and wellness.

Project: LEMONADE SALE

Description: Run a lemonade stand in your library with the proceeds benefiting H2O for Life (https://www.h2oforlifeschools.org/).

Community Partners: Lemonade is fairly easy to make, but you could consult a school cooking teacher for pointers or recipes with a twist! Include a teacher of environmental science to discuss water security.

Materials Needed: Pitchers, cups; a favorite lemonade recipe; this could be a research opportunity.

Instructions: Prior to event, your participants will need to advertise and promote the sale and perhaps build a signage or a stand. On day of the sale, prepare the lemonade. Remind teens to wash hands and other sanitary practices.

Doing More: When you set up your lemonade stand, display a container of dirty water with a signage explaining water insecurity and its effects. Your teens can also demonstrate water purification techniques as described above. While raising funds, capitalize on this opportune teachable moment. Water purification kits can be purchased for a nominal fee at Proctor & Gamble's Children's Safe Drinking Water (CSDW) program website at www .csdw.org/csdw/purifying-water-at-home.shtml. A portion of the purchase price is donated to the CSDW fund.

When: July is National Water Month and a typically hot summer month—a perfect time to quench your thirst for knowledge and serving!

Clothing

Project: LITTLE DRESSES FOR AFRICA (www.littledressesforafrica.org/blog/)

Community Partners: Do you have a sewing class at your school or a sewing circle at your public library? Working together with groups like this can make huge difference in quantity and quality of the dresses you can make and donate. Coordinate and collaborate with the Family and Consumer Science educator in your town. They will know who can sew, have access to machines, and can provide sewing mentors for your program. Another group sending pillowcase dresses around the world is Hope 4 Women International as part of its Dress a Girl Around the World campaign. The specifications for its dresses can be found on its website at www.dressagirlaroundtheworld.com/. Fabric, instead of pillowcases, is used to create dresses for this organization. Compare requirements for both and see which one suits your youth group's ability and other considerations.

Materials Needed: Pillowcase, double-fold bias tape, ¼-inch elastic, thread, sewing machines; embellishments such as pockets and lace may be added if you have confident participants.

Instructions: Go to the website listed above for sewing patterns and shipping address.

Menstrual Hygiene Management

Project: FEMININE HYGIENE KIT

Description: Lack of sanitary supplies keeps young girls from attending school, and many drop out altogether. While we may find

this unfathomable, girls in countries around the world do not have access to sanitary products like we do and are forced to make difficult decisions regarding their education. Girls suffer from interrupted learning, humiliation, and discomfort from using the only available products such as corn husks and newspapers. Dignity in menstrual hygiene management allows girls the opportunity of full-time education without weeks and months of their schooling interrupted. Many girls drop out of school altogether once menstruation commences. Your sewing group can put an end to this by sewing fabric sanitary napkins. These washable pads allow young girls to attend school full-time.

Community Partners: Little Dresses for Africa (www.littledressesforafrica.org/blog/) or Days for Girls (www.daysforgirls.org/). You may want to partner with sewing clubs in public libraries or sewing teachers in high schools to have access to more sewing machines and expertise.

Instructions: Patterns on each site are free. Kits are delivered to girls in over 100 countries. Little Dresses for Africa instructions can be found at http://www.littledressesforafrica.org/blog/sani-panti-sewing-instructions/.

Days for Girls: Free registration at https://www.daysforgirls.org/chaptersandteams for access to pattern. Patterns are available to registered chapter/team leaders.

Caveat: While the pattern is not overly difficult, quality matters, and therefore this project is recommended for more confident sewers with machine experience. Also, due to the nature of the items and their use, it is best discussed with older girls and boys who can understand and comprehend the issues involved.

Literacy and Cultural Diversity

Since many of you reading this book are probably librarians and other educators, a few literacy-related projects are included as well. So many ideas and situations open up to us from the books we read. Choosing, sharing, and reading books with culturally diverse characters, we learn and reflect on new cultures and explore people both different and similar to ourselves, whether socioeconomic status, race, ethnicity, religion, or ability. By encouraging youth to read diverse titles empathy and awareness develop.

Project: #WENEEDDIVERSEBOOKS—CULTURAL AWARENESS, ENGINEERING, INNOVATION, EDUCATION THROUGH GLOBAL THEMED BOOKS
Reading Group: *The Boy Who Harnessed the Wind*

While there is no specific make and donate opportunity here, participants can learn more about the continent of Africa, its needs, and concerns. Awareness is the first step to making a difference in a cause. The more we choose book club and Big Read titles with diverse themes, the more empathy and insight youth will develop. When we don't know that a problem or place exists, it tends to get overlooked. Students at Islip High School, New York, participated in a Big Read centered around William Kamkwambe's memoir, *The Boy Who Harnessed the Wind*. A section of the library was temporarily turned into a "town garbage dump" where students could scavenge for items to make windmills and water pumps just like William. This activity brought attention to the infrastructure situation in Africa. Electricity and running water are not always available. William's story also discusses his inability to continue his education as his parents lacked the funds for his school fees after a devastating drought hit their community in 2001. This also brings to light the education system in other countries as well as global food supply, food insecurity, and water supply. This story touches upon so many civic topics and is well worth the read. William is the ultimate example of civic engagement. He saw a problem, had no access to electricity, and then set out to change things first in his own home and then for his entire community. The community also benefited from William's irrigation system to water crops alleviating food shortages ensuring food supply for the community. William has been successful in creating the Moving Windmills group (www.movingwindmills.org/) to help other villages.
Instructions: Implement a Big Read or Book Club and read about William Kamkwambe; there are several versions of his book, picture book, young adult version, and adult book. While reading his story, learn about Africa, Malawi, both geography and culture. Be sure to implement a maker activity, too: perhaps a windmill, water pump, or just tinker like William!
Doing More: Youth can organize a maker fair or craft fair with proceeds benefiting William's organization, Moving Windmills. See the introduction to service projects for more ideas.

While we are on the subject of Big Reads, at Islip High School we also read *I Am Malala: The Girl Who Stood Up for Education and Was Shot by the Taliban*, another diverse cultural reading selection. Malala's story, like William's, stresses the importance of access to education, something many of our youth cannot comprehend. In William's case, he was denied access to school due to a lack of approximately $70 in yearly school fees. Malala was threatened because the Taliban were determined that girls should not be educated nor attend schools in Pakistan. We hosted numerous activities in the library to bring attention to Malala's story and culture. We even used our makerspace and button machine to make buttons in support of the #StandwithMalala campaign, which were worn throughout the school. Students designed their own buttons using quotes, pictures of Malala, and other decorations to make personalized buttons, bringing about awareness to a global cause of a child's right to an education. Adding another global element, we exchanged these handmade buttons with our book club buddies in London, England.

Project: #STANDWITHMALALA CAMPAIGN

Instructions: Implement a Big Read or Book Club and read about Malala; there are several versions of her book, picture book, young adult version, and adult book. Many of the versions are available in other languages, so be inclusive. Using a button-making machine, have youth design and make buttons with the hashtag Stand with Malala. Pick a convenient day to initiate a Stand with Malala Day where everyone dons his or her buttons in support and awareness of a child's right to an education.

Modifications: If you don't have a button maker, create posters to hang around your facility. A personalized digital poster generator can be found at http://www.stand withmalala.org/.

Doing More: Those looking for a vast annotated bibliography of children's and youth literature related to world issues should consult Cathryn Berger Kaye's *The Complete Guide to Service Learning: Proven, Practical Ways to Engage Students in Civic Responsibility, Academic Curriculum, and Social Action* (2010). The pairing of books to your projects, perhaps in a passive display, could prove useful to attracting more youth to your program or encouraging youth to dig deeper into a topic.

Handmade buttons to be worn.

BUILDING GLOBAL AWARENESS AND RELATIONSHIPS

Project: INTERNATIONAL SCHOOL LIBRARY MONTH BOOKMARK EXCHANGE

Description: A fun, creative way to make new friends in schools worldwide.

Community Partners: The International Association of School Librarianship celebrates International School Library Month (October) every year by matching school libraries for a bookmark exchange. In 2016, over 450 schools worldwide participated, with nearly 30,000 students participating from 29 countries. Schools are matched in August or September as the bookmarks need to be shipped out in October. You must register to be matched with a school or you can find a school, on your own through social networking. This latter option is a helpful option particularly if October is a busy month for your school library.

Materials Needed: Cardstock paper in a variety of colors, stamps, stickers, colored pencils, upcycled magazines or wallpaper, origami paper; the possibilities are endless so use whatever you have on hand. Single hole punch and yarn or ribbon if you wish to embellish the bookmark with a tassel. Beads can even be added to the end of the tassel. It's up to your craft supply and the creativity of youth that will guide this project. See Chapter 8 for numerous bookmark suggestions.

Caveat: When shipping items to partner schools overseas, you'll need to fill out a customs declaration form. Opt for lighter bookmarks to stretch your postal budget.

Project: THE HUGS BEAR PROJECT

Description: At first glance one might think this project should go in the chapter on military-related projects as these items are placed in care packages for deployed troops. However, this project benefits our military in that they build a better relationship and image with youth overseas. The overall purpose of this project is to create toys to be given to children in Iraq and Afghanistan in an act of kindness overseas.

Community Partners: The Hugs Project, sewing groups in your community.

Materials Needed: Fabric, needle, thread. Bear pattern. Can be hand stitched or use a sewing machine. The Hugs Project also provides free patterns for cool ties and helmet coolers (http://www.thehugsproject.com/bear-pattern-and-story/), projects discussed in the military section of this book as those projects mentioned directly benefit armed forces' personnel.

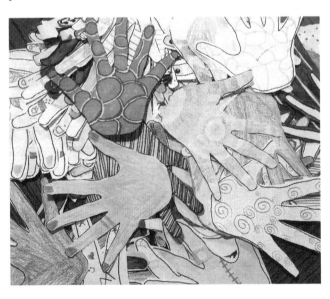

2017 Hand Challenge.

Project: STUDENTS REBUILD YEARLY CHALLENGE

Description: Students Rebuild, founded in 2010 and supported by the Bezos Family Foundation, establishes yearly challenges to raise funds and awareness on a variety of global issues. Through these symbolic art projects, students can make a significant philanthropic impact.

Instructions: Check its website for current campaign: http://studentsrebuild.org. My students participated in the Youth Uplift Challenge in 2017 by making and decorating paper hands. For each hand we made and mailed in, $1.90 was donated to Save the Children Foundation. It was a simple-to-implement project, raising funds and awareness. Each year a new challenge is selected, and Students Rebuild chooses new partner agencies. Past challenges have included creating pinwheels, flower garlands, bookmarks, and origami cranes. Each item represented a cause or situation in various respective countries. For example, the origami cranes raised funds for Japanese earthquake and tsunami relief in 2011. You'll want to work with this organization year after year!

FOOD INSECURITY

Food collection drives are one way to provide food for your community. Collection bins are often spotted in our schools, libraries, and town facilities. These efforts greatly affect those in need locally. We often are asked to collect funds for providing food donations globally. However, a group of South African schoolgirls went a little further and worked together to help improve food security in their region by building a satellite. Now that's civic engagement that's out of this world!

The girls designed and made the payload for the African continent's first private satellite by first programming and launching smaller satellites using high-altitude weather balloons. The teens took part in a STEM boot camp and were mentored by engineers from Cape Peninsula University of Technology; the satellite itself was purchased by South Africa's Meta Economic Development Organisation (MacDonald 2016). By programming the satellite payloads, thermal imaging data will be collected and will help identify where drought and floods are likely to occur (MacDonald 2016). The launch is scheduled for May 2017. Young people around the globe are an effective and valuable resource waiting to change their communities throughout the world. Here are a few ideas to get your group participating in addressing global food insecurity:

Project: FORM AN ONLINE GROUP IN FREE RICE (http://freerice.com)
Description: Free Rice will donate ten grains of rice for each correct answer given by youth and even adults playing the online quiz game. The more you play and the more players in your group, the more rice will be donated. Free Rice originally started with vocabulary quiz flash cards, but it now includes numerous subjects such as geography, humanities, chemistry, math, human anatomy, world languages, even SAT prep. The site and quiz activities can be accessed in English, French, Italian, Spanish, and Korean, so for schools and public libraries with immigrant populations the site allows for inclusive participation. The website includes educator support where one can find free digital artwork for marketing and ideas on working with students. Great way for kids to feed the world with rice while feeding their brains with knowledge.
Materials Needed: Internet access, PCs, laptops, tablets, or iPads enough for your group.
Instructions: Use your makerspace's laptops, tablets, or iPads to access the Free Rice website (http://freerice.com). Free Rice is a nonprofit agency that supports the UN World Food Program in providing free rice to hungry people throughout the world. Have kids access the site individually or better still create your own group on the site; online groups can be closed or open as you choose. Top ranking groups are noted weekly on the site.
Doing More: Have youth decorate rice-shaped cutouts with facts about world hunger and food insecurity. Display "rice" for a public awareness campaign in your library.

Start with a collection drive.

Project: READ TO FEED BOOK SALE

Description: Heifer International (https://www.heifer.org/) is an organization dedicated to ending hunger and poverty. Host a used book sale, Read to Feed, with book sales benefiting Heifer International. Heifer addresses learning about hunger, food supply, self-sufficiency, removing oneself from poverty by empowering recipients, by working with communities, and providing livestock and training for the livestock and farming projects to ensure success.

Instructions: Collect gently used books through donations. Youth organize the donations on book carts for sale, hence Read to Feed. In addition to selling the books, youth can use makerspace to design and make decorative bookmarks for sale and distribution during the event. The proceeds benefit Heifer International in its efforts to end world hunger.

GLOBAL WASTE AND CLIMATE CHANGE

Bring awareness to the issue of global waste and its effect on climate change by encouraging your community to upcycle common items they throw out. While the project items are not delivered abroad to be given to various communities, the creation and use of the T-shirt bags reduces waste that threatens our environment, which is a global issue. The United States is the leader of solid waste production at 624,700 metric tons a day. Each year, all nations combined generate 1.3 billion tons of waste, and with the projected expectation this number will increase to 4 billion tons by the year 2100 (Simmons 2016).

Project: NO-SEW T-SHIRT BAGS

Materials: Upcycled T-shirts, scissors. Optional: beads.

Instructions: Lay shirt flat on a table. Cut off sleeves on both sides of the shirt. Next make a U-shape cut at the shirt's collar. Cut 1–2-inch strips at the bottom of the shirt in ½-inch intervals. If you want a bag with fringes the shirt should be right-side out. If you want a bag without fringes, the shirt should be inside out. Tie off the fringes one at a time with a knot. The bag is done when you've tied the last fringe. If available, youth can slide the decorative beads on the fringe and tie off if desired. Decorative beads tied on the fringes are optional. You now have a two-handled recycled bag to use cutting down on plastic and clothing being added to our landfills. Protect our environment through sustainable living. It is a great project to bring awareness to garbage crisis and climate change. This project makes an excellent choice for sale at a charity craft fair. With proceeds benefiting a cause or charity of choice and little to no outlay of funds to create the items being sold, this is solely profit to donate.

Doing More: Carbon Footprint Calculator (https://www3.epa .gov/carbon-footprint-calculator/) found on the U.S. Environmental Protection Agency's website is a good introduction to issue. Host an Earth Day celebration.

MEDICAL ISSUES

Project: SOLE HOPE SHOE CUTTING PARTY (http://sole-hope.org/)

Description: It's hard to imagine not having shoes—not one pair! But there are many who go without and suffer the consequences. Sole Hope is a group that provides shoes and medical treatment to Ugandans suffering from jiggers. Jiggers are a parasite that affects barefoot persons in Uganda and elsewhere. These parasites burrow into unprotected feet and lay their eggs, which in turn multiply, cause damage to skin, and can lead to infections and other diseases. Your group can host a *party with a purpose*—a shoe-cutting party.

In this project, everyone can serve a function. Some will donate the supplies you need to cut out the patterns, others can sponsor the project through donated funds, and others will serve by cutting out the patterns to be shipped overseas. Sole Hope needs funds to ship your cut shoe pieces to Uganda where they employ local tailors and shoemakers to complete the process using a few additional supplies including glue and thread that need to be purchased in addition to locally upcycled tires to produce the sole of the shoes. Medical treatment is also factored into the suggested donation per shoe. Encourage youth to raise the funds themselves by skipping an afternoon treat at the local coffee shop, or they may ask the community, family, or friends to raise the funds. This latter option also raises awareness of this preventable debilitating medical condition.

Materials Needed: The shoe party kit is available on its online store (starting at $15); this includes the master pattern, instructional booklet, DVD, and other items. You'll also need denim material (upcycle this organizing a collection drive or go to a thrift store and purchase the largest-size pants you can find), scissors, Sharpies, pens, large safety pins, thin plastic (upcycled from milk jugs or other plastic container), and gallon-sized baggies.

Instructions: Gather your group and the supplies needed, watch the DVD supplied, and read the instructional booklet. Using a Sharpie marker trace out the pattern on the back of the material using the master pattern you received in your kit on the denim and plastic your group collected. Trace the patterns carefully or the shoe size will be off! When all shoe pieces have been cut, pin a pair of shoes together using one safety pin then ship your items to Sole Hope. The cost of shipping will vary depending on the number of shoes your group made and the location of your group. If you happen to live in North Carolina, you can drop off the items.

Doing More: Not required but your group can also run a collection drive for foot washing and jigger removal supplies needed. It's not enough to receive new shoes; the parasites must be removed, and proper foot hygiene is required. Some of the supplies needed include large safety pins, surgical gloves, cotton balls, antibiotic cream, gauze and Band-Aids. Check Sole Hope's website for needed supplies and where to ship them. During the collection drive, requests for donations can be solicited as $10 is the requested sponsorship for each shoe. Though these funds are not required, they are essential.

FAIR TRADE ADVOCACY AND ECONOMIC SECURITY

The Pulsera Project

Though it's not a service project for your youth to make, the Pulsera Project shows how youth in other countries are empowered as artists as fair trade practices are implemented. *Pulsera* is the Spanish word for bracelet. These handwoven bracelets are sold by youth groups across the United States bringing awareness to fair trade practices and workers' rights, and this project also supports education and financial empowerment.

KidKnits

Your purchases can improve the daily lives of impoverished struggling communities. Yarn purchased through KidKnits enables women in Rwanda and Chile to earn income and provide for their families. Curriculum is available on the KidKnits websites providing youth leaders with a convenient way to discuss poverty, countries and cultures different from our own, how change matters, and the effects of change on a community.

Human Trafficking/Economic Security

Community Partner: Free the Girls, service clubs, women's groups, social studies teacher teaching this topic.

Materials Needed: Collection receptacle and signs advertising and bringing awareness to the cause. Youth-decorated laundry baskets are an option.

Instructions: Set up a collection drive for gently used bras. Youth research and share relevant information along with the decorated receptacle for the donations.

Doing More: To piggyback on some of the above projects, notably Little Dresses for Africa or Feminine Hygiene Kit, consider pairing either activity with a gently used bra collection benefiting the Free the Girls (https://freethegirls.org/) organization. This group provides economic opportunities for victims of human trafficking in three countries: El Salvador, Mozambique, and Uganda. Survivors of trafficking can start a new life by selling your donated gently used bras on the secondhand market in their respective countries. Celebrate International Women's Day by helping women worldwide. While International Women's Day celebrates the social, cultural, economic, and political accomplishments of women, we can use this day to help and empower a girl or woman who has the potential to make such a contribution to society. You may not wish to tackle sensitive topics with certain groups, but most high school teens research global issues for school assignments and may be already familiar with this topic. For others, this could be an opportunity for personal growth and awareness. Human trafficking is a global issue, and there needs to be awareness to end this form of slavery. Through this program, former victims of human trafficking become entrepreneurs. Turn your group into modern-day abolitionists! Bring awareness to the horrific practice of human trafficking and sexual exploitation.

WAR, REFUGEES, AND INTERNALLY DISPLACED PERSONS

Knitters and crocheters can participate in the *afghans for Afghans* (http://www.afghans forafghans.org/) program benefiting infant mortality and internally displaced persons by making handmade blankets, socks, mittens, and baby hats given to Afghani relief agencies, when possible. It's best to check with this organization and indeed any organization operating in conflict areas prior to commencing your project. Occasionally, afghans for Afghans and other groups must suspend services when difficulty in securing transportation arises. At such times, these organizations do not accept donations as it is costly enough to hold onto their current supplies awaiting shipment and distribution. Additionally, these organizations have specific needs and so do not send unrequested items. Organizations working with relief agencies overseas, particularly those in conflict areas, have to abide by specific rules and requests. Do not assume your additional donation will be helpful, culturally appropriate, or accepted as cargo space is often limited. Always strictly follow the organization's guidelines as they best know the country and people and what could potentially be culturally insensitive. They know the climate and which fabrics and yarns are most suitable. They've researched this on your behalf, so take heed. Organizations handling internally displaced persons and refugees function better with cash donations. If this is an area your group wishes to support, it's best to host a craft sale with proceeds benefiting a youth-chosen organization. During your event, youth can spread awareness of the situation to promote additional aid given among community members. As part of your DIY craft sale, youth can use the makerspace supplies to create posters and flyers educating craft fair attendees. This scenario offers a good mix of traditional library research and library makerspace supplies in support of a cause.

Project: KNITTING WITHOUT BORDERS BEARS
Description: Handmade knitted and crocheted bears are sent to orphanages, schools, and hospitals in Africa, Asia, the Caribbean, Central America, Europe, North America, and South America.
Community Partners: Knitting Without Borders, knitting and crocheting groups.
Materials Needed: Yarn, knitting needles size 7 or 8, crochet hook F or G, needle and thread, pattern. Knitting Without Borders pattern instructions (www.knittingwithoutbor ders.jigsy.com/pattern) are available in English, Spanish, and Italian for your limited English language proficient participants.
Instructions: Using the pattern, knit a bear, stuff with Poly-Fil, and sew together. Check its website for current mailing address.
Caveat: Teddy bears are approximately 7 inches; do not make them larger as it makes shipping them more burdensome and costly. Also, don't use anything but yarn and Poly-Fil as buttons and other objects pose a choking hazard.

DISASTER RELIEF

Innovation is not just occurring in company workrooms or suburban garages. Innovative thinking and design is essential in the field, and humanitarian organizations are on the forefront. Participation in disaster relief is not a library makerspace project, nor is it available to teen volunteers. However, it is possible that one day your youth will join a nongovernmental organization (NGO) and use a 3D printer on foreign soil. As maker mentors, we are inspiring a next generation of change agents, volunteers, and community workers. Some of the skills youth learn in school, in a makerspace, and possibly from service activities will prepare them for work with an NGO providing aid around the world. 3D printing has become an asset in crisis areas allowing the creation of needed parts to be individually and uniquely fashioned versus waiting for a delivery of a part that may fit. This type of printing on the fly provides maximum benefit in both time and cost as it revolutionizes the supply chain (Jones 2015; Halterman 2015). Field Ready, a humanitarian organization with an emphasis on technology in disaster relief, makes 3D files available for download on Thingiverse, including various medical and surgical clamps, nebulizer fittings, and IV bag hook. Through direct immediate intervention, humanitarian resources and services can be applied directly where needed without waste or delay. Think about the youth you work with. They are the future to providing aid both home and away.

CONCLUSION

Hopefully this book has inspired you to action. After you have tried a few of the projects in this book, be sure to share your experiences with other youth leaders. So many causes, so many makers! And as we know, many hands make light work. So go forth and make a difference!

Appendix A: Communication Templates

Here's what you can say when initiating a partnership, seeking a donation, or saying thank-you.

PARTNERSHIP INQUIRY (PHONE OR E-MAIL)

Be friendly, state your name, and whom you represent. Briefly explain how you can assist the organization. Here's where you should be familiar with the mission of the organization. Viewing their website and social media accounts will give you insight into the group, their potential needs, and how you can help. Do some research prior to contact.

Example:

Hello, my name is *Gina Seymour* and I'm the *school librarian* at *Islip High School*. I work with teens who want to make a difference by creating items to donate to local organizations like *Name the Organization*. [*Briefly explain what you can do (for example, woodworking, 3D printing, or knitting).*] Would you be interested in the items mentioned or do you have other needs at this time? We look forward to hearing from you.

Follow-up should always include specifics and queries to any special requirements that must be adhered to.

When initiating a phone call, begin with the example above. Then, remember to pause and listen. Listening and being receptive to the organization's needs will ensure a productive partnership. You need to give the organization the opportunity to share their needs or concerns. They don't have to be grateful because you're offering something they don't need. Don't talk at someone; talk with them.

DONATION LETTER/E-MAIL/SOCIAL MEDIA POST

XYZ library group is working on *name of project* (describe in a few words if the title is not self-evident) to benefit *whom is this going to or helping* and we need the following items: *list what you need*. If you have any of these items, please drop off at *give specific clear location*. Any questions contact *name* at *either a phone number or e-mail*. Thanks!

Example:

Students at Islip High School are working on making braided T-shirt dog toys to be donated to the Town of Islip Animal Shelter and we need your used, no longer needed T-shirts. If you can donate old T-shirts, please drop them off at the Main Office at Islip High School. Any questions, please contact Mrs. Seymour at gseymour@islipufsd.org. Thank you.

THE PARTNERSHIP THANK-YOU LETTER

Example:

Dear *Organization/Staff Member Name*,

Students/youth members of *name of school/service club* were so pleased to provide your *organization name*, with *describe the donation*. (Describe the experience, if appropriate.) Our teens were so moved by this experience. (You can ask youth to reflect on their actions and use a few quotes in this letter.) We look forward to a continued partnership in helping *name of organization* provide *state the mission of the organization*.

Sincerely,
Your Group Name

THE DONATION THANK-YOU LETTER

You don't need to individually thank every donor particularly when requesting upcycled supplies such as plastic bags. A verbal thank-you or a shout-out on social media is acceptable and appreciated. However, if someone goes above the average donation a note of thanks is warranted.

Dear *Person/Family Name*,

On behalf of the *XYZ Youth Group*, we'd like to extend our thanks for your generous donation of *name the item(s)*. These items have allowed us to create *name item* that were donated to *name of organization* earlier this *month/week*. (State how the finished product is helpful. Add a quote or two from youth participants.) Thank you for your support.

Sincerely,
XYZ Youth Group

Appendix B: Calendar of Related Dates and Celebrations

This appendix includes celebrations promoting service days or projects highlighted included in this book.

JANUARY

Martin Luther King Day of Service (Third Monday of January)
http://www.nationalservice.gov/mlkday
The Rev. Dr. Martin Luther King Jr. federal holiday is a perfect opportunity for Americans to honor Dr. King's legacy through service. The MLK Day of Service empowers individuals, strengthens communities, bridges barriers, creates solutions to social problems, and moves us closer to Dr. King's vision of a beloved community.

FEBRUARY

National Random Acts of Kindness Day (February 17)
https://www.randomactsofkindness.org/
Observed on February 17, National Random Acts of Kindness Day has grown in popularity each year. It is celebrated by individuals, groups, and organizations nationwide to encourage acts of kindness.

Souper Bowl of Caring
https://souperbowl.org/
This event is aimed at fighting hunger and poverty in America in the weeks approaching the Super Bowl football game.

National Salute to Veteran Patients Week (The week of February 14)
http://www.volunteer.va.gov/NationalSaluteVeteranPatients.asp
It is show your appreciation to veterans and highlight the work performed by VA medical centers.

Make a Blanket Day (Third Saturday of February)
This event is sponsored by Project Linus, though you can make a blanket for any cause.

American Heart Month (February)

National Green Week (Choose a convenient week between the first full week in February through April 30)
http://www.greeneducationfoundation.org/greenweek.html
Schools and youth groups are encouraged to engage in sustainability projects and promote sustainability awareness. Many of the projects in this book utilize upcycled materials.

MARCH

International Women's Day (March 8)
http://www.internationalwomensday.com/

AmeriCorps Week (Begins first Saturday of the month)
http://www.nationalservice.gov/programs/americorps/americorps-week

Youth Art Month
http://www.arteducators.org/news/yam

Teen Tech Week (Second week of March)
http://teentechweek.ning.com/
Sponsored by YALSA (Young Adult Library Services Association).

National Green Week (Choose a convenient week between the first full week in February through April 30)
http://www.greeneducationfoundation.org/greenweek.html
Schools and youth groups are encouraged to engage in sustainability projects and promote sustainability awareness. Many of the projects in this book utilize upcycled materials.

APRIL

Random Acts of Kindness Endure for Kindness (E4K)
http://www.randomacts.org/events/endure4kindness
It is a global event where participants are challenged to participate in an activity continuously for 24 hours.

Global Youth Service Day (Dates vary)
http://ysa.org/act/programs/gysd
"Youth-led solutions to real-world problems." It is the largest day of service event and sponsored by Youth Service America (YSA).

Good Deeds Day (Dates vary)
http://www.good-deeds-day.org
A "global movement of doing good."

Upcoming dates (occasionally celebrated at the end of March):

Good Deeds Day 2019 will take place on April 7.
Good Deeds Day 2020 will take place on March 29.

National Volunteer Week (Dates vary)
http://www.pointsoflight.org/signature-events/national-volunteer-week
Future National Volunteer Week dates:

April 7–13, 2019
April 19–25, 2020
April 18–24, 2021

Every Kid Healthy Week (Last week of April)
http://www.everykidhealthyweek.org/
It highlights the importance of health and wellness in students through nutrition and physical activity because healthy children learn better.

Areyvut National Mitzvah Day (Date varies; usually first Sunday of April)
http://www.areyvut.org/areyvut_in_action/national_mitzvah_day/

National Autism Awareness Month
http://www.autism-society.org/get-involved/national-autism-awareness-month/

National Library Week (Second full week of April)
http://www.ala.org/conferencesevents/celebrationweeks/natlibraryweek

J-serve (Dates vary)
http://www.jserve.org/
Day of service for Jewish teens globally.

Earth Day (April 22)
http://www.earthday.org/

National Green Week (Choose a convenient week between the first full week in February through April 30)
http://www.greeneducationfoundation.org/greenweek.html
Schools and youth groups are encouraged to engage in sustainability projects and promote sustainability awareness. Many of the projects in this book utilize upcycled materials.

MAY

Lost Sock Memorial Day (May 9)
Use up those lost socks making projects such as Upcycled Catnip Sock Toys.

World Migratory Bird Day (May 10)

National Foster Care Month
https://www.childwelfare.gov/fostercaremonth/

National Physical Fitness and Sports Month

Older Americans Month
https://oam.acl.gov/

Join Hands Day (First Saturday of May)
http://www.generationon.org/orgs/join_hands_day
This day is set aside for youth and adults to work together in service.

Be Kind to Animals Week (First week)
http://www.kindness100.org/

World Fair Trade Day (Second Saturday of May)
http://wfto.com/events/world-fair-trade-day-2017

JUNE

International Children's Day (June 1)

World Refugee Day (June 20)
www.worldrefugeeday.us

Gay and Lesbian Pride Month
www.glsen.org

World Environment Day (June 5)
http://www.unep.org/wed

Yarn Bombing Day (June 11)
https://www.daysoftheyear.com/days/yarn-bombing-day/

JULY

National Water Month

National Craft for Your Local Shelter Day (July 21)

AUGUST

Senior Citizens Day (August 21)

International Youth Day (August 12)
http://www.un.org/en/events/youthday/

National Relaxation Day (August 15)

National Dog Day (August 26)

SEPTEMBER

National Teddy Bear Day (September 9)

September 11th National Day of Service and Remembrance (September 11)
http://www.serve.gov/?q=site-page/september-11th-national-day-service-and-remembrance
On the anniversary of the September 11 terrorist attacks, Americans use this day to come together in ser-
    vice of others to remember the lives of those lost, pay tribute to those who rose in service, and honor
    those who continue to serve our country today.

Roald Dahl Day (September 13, Roald Dahl's Birthday)
http://www.roalddahl.com/create-and-learn/join-in/roald-dahl-day
This celebration is for anything related to Roald Dahl. Use famous quotes such as "Somewhere inside all
    of us is the power to change the world" from his book *Matilda* to mark this celebration.

International Dot Day (September 15)
http://www.thedotclub.org/dotday/
Join the growing global community of creativity champions using their talents, gifts, and energy to move
    the world to a better place.

Hunger Action Month
http://www.feedingamerica.org/take-action/campaigns/hunger-action-month.html

International Literacy Day (September 8)
http://www.unesco.org/new/en/unesco/events/prizes-and-celebrations/celebrations/international-days/
    literacy-day/

International Day of Peace (September 21)
http://internationaldayofpeace.org/

OCTOBER

Make a Difference Day
http://makeadifferenceday.com/

Breast Cancer Awareness Month

Domestic Violence Awareness Month
http://www.nrcdv.org/dvam/DVAM-history

World Habitat Day (First Monday in October)
http://www.habitat.org/getinv/events/world-habitat-day
It recognizes the importance of shelter. Think global, act local with your community Habitat for Hu-
    manity office.

World Cerebral Palsy Day (October 6)
https://worldcpday.org/

World Mental Health Day (October 10)
http://www.who.int/mental_health/world-mental-health-day/en/

I Love Yarn Day (October 15)
http://www.craftyarncouncil.com/I-Love-Yarn

Teen Read Week (Second week of October)
http://teenreadweek.ning.com/

World Food Day (October 16)
http://www.un.org/en/events/habitatday/

Kiwanis One Day (Fourth Saturday in October)
http://www.kiwanis.org/clubs/member-resources/service-projects/kiwanis-one-day#.VbfOs_lViko
It is a day of service organized by the Kiwanis Club.

NOVEMBER

America Recycles Day (November 15)
https://americarecyclesday.org/
While this isn't a specific volunteer or service celebration, it can be coupled with a service project that
   utilizes upcycled items.

Veteran's Day (November 11)

National Hunger and Homelessness Awareness Week (Week prior to Thanksgiving)
https://hhweek.org/

World Diabetes Day (November 14)
http://www.idf.org/wdd-index

World Kindness Day (November 13)
https://www.randomactsofkindness.org/

National Family Volunteer Day (November 18)
http://www.pointsoflight.org/signature-events/family-volunteer-day

DECEMBER

International Day of Persons with Disabilities (December 3)
http://www.timeanddate.com/holidays/un/international-day-persons-disabilities
A global observance organized by the United Nations.

International Volunteer Day (December 5)
http://www.volunteeractioncounts.org/en/

Human Rights Day (December 10)
http://www.un.org/en/events/humanrightsday/

National Letter Writing Day (December 7)

Appendix C: List of National Organizations

Action Book Club, program of the Little Free Library
http://littlefreelibrary.org/actionbookclub/
573 Co. Rd. A, Suite 106
Hudson, WI 54016
Phone: 715–690–2488
Fax: 715–690–2491

afghans for Afghans
http://www.afghansforafghans.org/
P.O. Box 475843
San Francisco, CA 94147–5843
E-mail: Afghans4Afghans@aol.com

American Red Cross: Red Cross Youth
http://redcrossyouth.org/
Red Cross Youth hosts a National Youth Involvement Month (#NYIM) during the month of November, a celebration dedicated to highlighting youth involvement throughout the country. About 20 percent of the entire Red Cross volunteer force comprises Red Cross youth. For Holiday for Heroes program, contact your local Red Cross office.

Appalachian Wildlife Refuge
http://www.appalachianwild.org/
P.O. Box 121
Skyland, NC 28776
E-mail: Info@AppalachianWild.org
Wands for Wildlife, collect upcycled mascara wands to aid animals.

Be a Noble Kid
http://www.beanoblekid.org
5120 Hungary Branch Court
Glen Allen, VA 23060
E-mail: info@beanoblekid.org

Beads of Courage
http://www.beadsofcourage.org/
3230 N. Dodge Blvd., Suite J
Tucson, AZ 85716
Phone: 520–344–7668
Fax: 520–344–7824

Blue Line Bears
http://bluelinebears.org/
Contact: http://bluelinebears.org/index.php/contact/

Build a Better Book Initiative
http://sciencediscovery.colorado.edu/program/buildabetterbook/
"Engaging youth in Makerspaces to create accessible picture books"
University of Colorado, Boulder
Science Learning Laboratory
3400 Marine Street, UCB 446
Boulder, CO 80309
Phone: 303–492–7188
Fax: 303–735–6443
E-mail (Stacey Forsyth, Director): stacey.forsyth@colorado.edu

The CAP Project
https://www.thecapproject.org/
E-mail: contact@thecapproject.org
Computer-aided pets project where volunteers are matched with animals needing assistive
devices. Site includes links to open-source 3D printable assistive devices and prosthetics.

Cases for Smiles
http://caseforsmiles.org/
295 E. Swedesford Rd. #396
Wayne, PA 19087
E-mail: melissa@caseforsmiles.org

Causes
http://www.causes.com/
Start an online campaign or fund-raiser using this site.

Color a Smile
http://colorasmile.org/
P.O. Box 1516
Morristown, NJ 07962–1516
Phone: 973–540–9222
E-mail: info@colorasmile.org

Corporation for National Service
https://www.nationalservice.gov/
It provides information on service learning projects, grants, and funding opportunities links as well.

Craft Yarn Council
3740 N. Josey Lane, Suite 102
Carrollton, TX 75007
Phone: 972–325–7232
Fax: 972–215–7333
It occasionally offers free yarn and crochet hooks or knitting needles. Instructions vary from basic to advanced. It also provides links for Spanish and French translations of yarn-related words.

The Danish Octo Project/Spruttegruppen
https://www.spruttegruppen.dk/danish-octo-project-english/
E-mail: danishoctos@spruttegruppen.dk
Instructions are available in English, British, Danish, Italian, and Spanish.

Days for Girls
http://www.daysforgirls.org/
1610 Grover Street, Suite B22
Lynden, WA 98264
Phone: 360–220–8393
info@daysforgirls.org
It is a nonprofit group working to provide sanitary supplies to girls in over 100 countries. Find free patterns for your volunteers to sew sanitary kits.

Doing Good Together
http://www.doinggoodtogether.org/
5141, 16th Avenue South
Minneapolis, MN 55417
Contact: http://www.doinggoodtogether.org/contact/

DoSomething.org
https://www.dosomething.org/us

Dress a Girl Around the World
http://www.dressagirlaroundtheworld.com/
C/o Hope 4 Women International
P.O. Box 8061
Tempe, AZ 85281
Phone: 480–392–1317

Enabling the Future
http://enablingthefuture.org/
Contact: info@enablingthefuture.org
Open-source 3D prosthetics.

Enchanted Makeovers
http://www.enchantedmakeovers.org/
12663 Hipp St.
Taylor, MI 48180
Phone: 1–855–743–4763
E-mail: EnchantedMakeovers@comcast.net
Crafts, sewing, knitting, and crocheting for homeless shelter makeovers. Also, Capes for Kids program.

Envision the Future Design Challenge
https://www.matterhackers.com/envisionthefuture
Annual challenge for youth 18 and under.

EPICS (Engineering Projects in Community Service)
https://engineering.purdue.edu/EPICS/EPICS/k12
The EPICS High Program at Purdue
Neil Armstrong Hall of Engineering
701 W. Stadium Avenue
West Lafayette, IN 47907–2045
Phone: 765–496–1068
Fax: 765–494–0052
E-mail: epics.high@purdue.edu
"EPICS is a service-learning design program in which teams of students partner with local and global community organizations to address human, community, and environmental needs."

Free Rice
http://freerice.com
E-mail: wfp.freerice@wfp.org

Free the Girls
https://freethegirls.org/
1552 Pioneer Trail
Chesterton, IN 46304
Phone: 720–383–4384
E-mail: info@freethegirls.org

Games for Change
http://www.gamesforchange.org/
205 E. 42nd St., 20th floor
New York, NY 10017
Phone: 212–242–4922
E-mail: contact@gamesforchange.org
"Catalyzing social impact through digital games."

GenerationOn

http://www.generationon.org
35 West 35th Street, 6th Floor
New York, NY 10001
Phone: 917–746–8182
E-mail: info@generationOn.org
GenerationOn, the youth division of Points of Light, is dedicated to providing programs and resources that support the development of caring, compassionate, and capable kids and teens, through service, empowering them to become change makers in their communities and the world.

Giving Artfully and Giving Artfully Kids

https://www.givingartfully.com/
Phone: 708–406–9278
E-mail: Gakids@givingartfully.com
It helps crafters find organizations needing handcrafted items and also provides crafting-based service learning curriculum where youth learn about giving and kindness.

Global Giving (crowdfunding site)

https://www.globalgiving.org/
1110 Vermont Ave. NW Suite 550
Washington DC 20005
Phone: 877–605–2314
Fax: 202–315–2558

Global Nomads Group

http://gng.org/home
132 Nassau St., Suite 822
New York, NY 10038
Phone: 212–529–0377
Using virtual reality technology, Global Nomads Group fosters dialogue and understanding among the world's youth. These experiences promote empathy and peace.

Habitat for Humanity

http://www.habitat.org
http://www.habitat.org/volunteer/near-you/youth-programs
Habitat for Humanity is a global nonprofit organization dedicated to housing issues. Youth may participate in various ways.

Heavenly Hats Foundation

http://heavenlyhats.org/
2325 Pamperin Rd. Suite 3
Green Bay, WI 54313
Phone: 920–362–2668
Fax: 920–469–1950

International Association of School Librarianship

http://www.iasl-online.org
http://www.iasl-online.org/advocacy/islm
Contact: http://www.iasl-online.org/contact
It hosts annual International School Library Month Bookmark Exchange.

International Rescue Committee
https://www.rescue.org/
122 East 42nd Street
New York, NY 10168–1289
Phone: 212–551–3000
Fax: 212–551–3179

Knots of Love
http://www.knotsoflove.org
2973 Harbor Blvd. #822
Costa Mesa, CA 92626
Phone: 949–933–7000
E-mail: info@knotsoflove.org
Patterns are available in English, Spanish, and Italian. Knots of Love provides free patterns of the following items: Chemotherapy caps, veterans' arm and leg stump covers, PICC line covers.

Landstuhl Hospital Care Project
http://www.landstuhlhospitalcareproject.org/
29 Greenleaf Terrace
Stafford, VA 22556
Contact: http://www.landstuhlhospitalcareproject.org/lhcp/contact/

Little Dresses for Africa
http://www.littledressesforafrica.org/blog/
24614 Curtis Dr.
Brownstown, MI 48134
Phone: 734–637–9064
Volunteers sew children's dresses made from pillowcases that are then shipped to Africa and distributed through mission teams to orphanages, churches, and schools. Pillowcase dress patterns are available on website. It also includes patterns for feminine hygiene kits.

Little Free Library
https://littlefreelibrary.org/
573 Co. Rd. A, Suite 106
Hudson, WI 54016
Phone: 715–690–2488
Fax: 715–690–2491

Matthew Freeman Project
http://freemanproject.org/
E-mail: info@freemanproject.org.

My Stuff Bag Foundation
http://www.mystuffbags.org/
5347 Sterling Center Drive
Westlake Village, CA 91361
Phone: 818–865–3860 or 866–3MY-STUFF (toll free)
Fax: 818–865–3865
Contact: http://www.mystuffbags.org/contact/
Bags are made for children in temporary housing, such as foster care, homeless shelters, or crisis shelters. This organization also accepts handmade single ply blankets. Blankets made for My Stuff should be single ply to make room for more "stuff" in the child's bag.

National Youth Leadership Council (NYLC)
https://nylc.org/
1667 Snelling Ave N
Saint Paul, MN 55108
Phone: 651–631–3672
E-mail: info@nylc.org

Operation Gratitude
https://opgrat.wordpress.com/
21100 Lassen Street
Chatsworth, CA 91311–4278
Phone: 262–674–7281
E-mail: Info@operationgratitude.com
Care packages filled with snacks, handmade items, and personal letters of appreciation are distributed for U.S. troops, new recruits, veterans, first responders, wounded warriors, caregivers, and to individually named U.S. service members deployed overseas.

The Peace Crane Project
https://peacecraneproject.org/
108 Por La Mar Circle
Santa Barbara CA 93103

Pledge Cents (crowdfunding platform)
https://www.pledgecents.com/
E-mail: info@pledgecents.com

Project Linus National Headquarters
http://www.projectlinus.org/
P.O. Box 1548
Belton, MO 64012–1108
Phone: 309–585–0686

Pulsera Project
http://www.pulseraproject.org/
It is a cultural, fair-trade, reciprocal service project. Youth in other countries make the pulseras (bracelets), and students here sell those bracelets and raise awareness.

Serve.gov: Corporation for National and Community Service
https://www.serve.gov/
E-mail: serviceinitiative@cns.gov

Sole Hope
http://solehope.org/
605 East Innes St. #3263
Salisbury, NC 28144
Phone: 855–516-HOPE (4673)
E-mail: support@solehope.org

Start Some Good
https://startsomegood.com/
E-mail: support@startsomegood.com
"Crowdfunding platform for changemakers."

StickTogether Products
https://www.letsticktogether.com/
E-mail: info@letsticktogether.com
It is a collaborative community-building activity. A coded grid of a pixelated image is filled in with thousands of colored stickers by group participants. Custom images can be ordered.

Students Rebuild
http://studentsrebuild.org
E-mail: info@studentsrebuild
Participate in the annual Youth Uplift Challenge.

Verizon Innovative Learning—App Challenge
https://appchallenge.tsaweb.org/
E-mail: appchallenge@tsaweb.org
It "is a nationwide contest in which middle and high school students are challenged to develop concepts for mobile apps that solve a problem in their community." See website for rules and registration.

Warm Up America
http://www.warmupamerica.org/
3740 N. Josey Lane, Suite 102
Carrollton, TX 75007
Phone: 972–325–7232
Fax: 972–215–7333
Contact: www.warmupamerica.org/contact-wua
Free crochet and knit patterns, downloadable lesson plans, posters, and more.

Warmth for Warriors
http://warmthforwarriors.com
P.O. Box 353
Rudyard, MI 49780
Phone: 906–478–4191
E-mail: warmth4warriors@gmail.com

Wildlife Rescue Nests
http://wildliferescuenests.weebly.com/
Contact: http://wildliferescuenests.weebly.com/contact-us.html
It is a network of volunteer crocheters and knitters who create handmade nests to licensed wildlife rescue and rehabilitation facilities worldwide.

The World We Want Foundation
http://theworldwewantfoundation.org; http://theworldwewantfoundation.org
20 Sunnyside Avenue, Suite 428
Mill Valley, CA 94941
E-mail: info@theworldwewantfoundation.org
Contact: http://theworldwewantfoundation.org/contact/
"Philanthropy for Young Global Citizens." "The World We Want Foundation promotes and supports young global citizens creating positive social change in their communities and around the world."

Youth Service America
http://ysa.org
Youth Service America (YSA) is an organization dedicated to helping young people take action. Grants are available.

Bibliography

Akande, Zainab. "People Are Knitting Cozy Little Nests for Rescued Baby Animals." The Dodo. Last modified February 22, 2016. Accessed December 4, 2016. https://www.thedodo.com/wildlife-rescue-nests-for-baby-animals-1618682839.html.

American Library Association. "Democracy Statement." American Library Association. Accessed July 6, 2017. http://www.ala.org/aboutala/governance/officers/past/kranich/demo/statement.

ASPCA. "Pet Statistics." ASPCA. Accessed May 13, 2017. https://www.aspca.org/animal-homelessness/shelter-intake-and-surrender/pet-statistics.

Balagna, Mary, and Carol Babbitt. *Quilt It with Love: The Project Linus Story: 20+ Quilt Patterns and Stories to Warm Your Heart.* New York: Lark Crafts, 2012.

Bell, Katherine. *Quilting for Peace: Make the World a Better Place One Stitch at a Time.* New York: Stewart, Tabori & Chang, 2009.

Bradford, Melanie. "Motivating Students through Project-Based Service Learning." *T.H.E. Journal* 32, no. 6 (January 2005): 29–30. Accessed December 5, 2016. ProQuest.

Byker, Erik John. *Like a Ripple on Water: An Impact Study of H20 for Life.* White Bear Lake, MN: H20 for Life, 2017.

Cerone, Lulu. *Philanthroparties!: A Party-planning Guide for Kids Who Want to Give Back.* New York: Aladdin, 2017.

Coppola, Carolyn. *Color for a Cause: A Coloring Book Made by High School Art Students.* Edited by Cristina Perez. Illustrated by Bernards High School Art Students. N.p.: CreateSpace Independent Publishing Platform, 2016.

Cornell Lab of Ornithology. "Window Collisions." All About the Birds. Accessed December 24, 2016. http://www.birds.cornell.edu/AllAboutBirds/attracting/challenges/window_collisions/document_view.

Cress, Christine M., Peter J. Collier, and Vicki L. Reitenauer. *Learning through Serving: A Student Guidebook for Service-learning and Civic Engagement across Academic Disciplines and Cultural Communities.* 2nd ed. Sterling, VA: Stylus, 2013.

Crowley, Brianna, and Barry Saide. "Building Empathy in Classrooms and Schools." *Education Week Teacher.* Last modified January 20, 2016. Accessed November 21, 2016. http://www.edweek.org/tm/articles/2016/01/20/building-empathy-in-classrooms-and-schools.html.

de los Reyes, Ignacio. "The Bolivian Women Who Knit Parts for Hearts." *BBC News*, March 29, 2015, Health. Accessed November 26, 2016. http://www.bbc.com/news/health-32076070.

DoSomething.org. "The DoSomething.org Index on Youth and Volunteering." Last modified 2012. Accessed January 4, 2017. https://www.dosomething.org/sites/default/files/blog/2012-Web-Singleview_0.pdf.

Dougherty, Dale. *Free to Make: How the Maker Movement Is Changing Our Schools, Our Jobs, and Our Minds.* Berkeley, CA: North Atlantic Books, 2016.

Duckworth, Angela. *Grit: The Power of Passion and Perseverance*. New York: Scribner, 2016.

Durrance, Joan C., Karen Pettigrew, Michael Jourdan, and Karen Scheuerer. "Libraries and Civil Society." In *Libraries and Democracy: The Cornerstones of Liberty*, edited by Nancy C. Kranich. Chicago: American Library Association, 2001. Accessed June 9, 2016. http://library-science.weebly.com/uploads/4/1/3/2/4132239/libraries__democracy.pdf.

"11 Facts about Hunger in the US." DoSomething.org. Accessed May 28, 2017. https://www.dosomething.org/facts/11-facts-about-hunger-us.

"FAQs." Ryan's Case for Smiles. Accessed February 6, 2017. http://caseforsmiles.org/faq/.

Fleming, Laura. *Worlds of Making: Best Practices for Establishing a Makerspace for Your School*. Thousand Oaks, CA: Corwin, a SAGE company, 2015.

Garber, Elizabeth. "Craft as Activism." *The Journal of Social Theory in Art Education* 33 (2013): 53–66. Accessed July 14, 2017. http://jerome.stjohns.edu:81/login?url=https://search-proquest-com.jerome.stjohns.edu/docview/1466173639?accountid=14068.

"Global Poverty." In *Taking on Inequality: Poverty and Shared Prosperity 2016*, 35–36. Washington, DC: World Bank Group, 2016. Accessed November 10, 2016. doi:10.1596/978-1-4648-0958-3.

Gonzalez, Angi. "Little Free Library Unveiled in St. George." *Spectrum News NY1*. Last modified August 22, 2015. Accessed May 16, 2017. http://www.ny1.com/nyc/staten-island/news/2015/08/22/little-free-library-unveiled-in-st—george.html.

Gray, Maryann J., Elizabeth H. Ondaatje, and Laura Zakaras. *Combining Service and Learning in Higher Education*. Santa Monica, CA: RAND Education, 1999. Accessed December 4, 2016. https://www.rand.org/content/dam/rand/pubs/monograph_reports/2005/MR998.1.pdf.

Greer, Betsy, ed. *Craftivism: The Art of Craft and Activism*. Vancouver: Arsenal Pulp Press, 2014.

Grimm, Robert, Jr., Nathan Dietz, Kimberly Spring, Kelly Arey, and John Foster-Bey. *Building Active Citizens: The Role of Social Institutions in Teen Volunteering*. Brief no. 1. November 2005. Accessed July 15, 2017. https://www.nationalservice.gov/pdf/05_1130_LSA_YHA_study.pdf.

Halterman, T. E. "Power to the People: 3D Printing Being Used in Disaster Relief." 3DPrint.com. Last modified April 6, 2015. Accessed April 11, 2017. https://3dprint.com/56149/3d-printing-disaster-relief/.

HIA Foundation. *The Academic Value of Hands-on Craft Projects in Elementary Schools*. Elmwood Park, NJ: Hobby Industry Association, 2002. Accessed November 16, 2016. https://www.home-school.com/news/summ.pdf.

I Can't Believe I'm Crocheting! Updated ed. Little Rock, AR: Leisure Arts, 2006.

Indiana Youth Institute. *Helping You—Helping Me: Why Youth Volunteering Matters*. July 2011. Accessed July 15, 2017. https://s3.amazonaws.com/iyi-website/issue-briefs/June-6-2011-Volunteering.pdf?mtime=20151110111102.

Jones, Sam. "When Disaster Strikes, It's Time to Fly in the 3D Printers." *The Guardian*. Last modified December 30, 2015. Accessed April 11, 2017. https://www.theguardian.com/global-development/2015/dec/30/disaster-emergency-3d-printing-humanitarian-relief-nepal-earthquake.

Karalyte, Egle. "What Is Design Thinking?" InfinVision. Accessed January 6, 2017. http://infinvision.com/design-thinking/.

Kaye, Cathryn Berger. *The Complete Guide to Service Learning: Proven, Practical Ways to Engage Students in Civic Responsibility, Academic Curriculum, and Social Action*. 2nd ed. Minneapolis, MN: Free Spirit Publishing, 2010.

Kilman, Carrie. "Lonely Language Learners." *Education Digest* 75, no. 2 (2009): 16–20. Academic Search Premier.

Kim, Helena. "The Sleeping Bag Project." *Craft Ideas* (2016): 96.

Kostakis, Vasilis, Vasilis Niaros, and Christos Giotitsas. "Open Source 3D Printing as a Means of Learning: An Educational Experiment in Two High Schools in Greece." *Telematics and Informatics* 32, no. 1 (February 2015): 118–28. http://dx.doi.org/10.1016/j.tele.2014.05.001.

Kravets, Lauren. "Cedar Park Students Make 3D Prosthetic Hand for Schoolmate." KXAN. Last modified February 2, 2017. Accessed March 6, 2017. http://kxan.com/2017/02/02/cedar-park-students-make-3d-prosthetic-hand-for-schoolmate/.

Lahey, Jessica. *The Gift of Failure: How the Best Parents Learn to Let Go So Their Children Can Succeed*. New York: Harper, an imprint of HarperCollins Publishers, 2015.

Lewis, Barbara A. *The Teen Guide to Global Action: How to Connect with Others (Near & Far) to Create Social Change*. Minneapolis, MN: Free Spirit, 2008.

Lewis, Barbara A., and Michelle Lee. *The Kid's Guide to Service Projects: Over 500 Service Ideas for Young People Who Want to Make a Difference*. 2nd ed. Minneapolis, MN: Free Spirit, 2009.

MacDonald, Fiona. "Teenage Girls Have Built Africa's First-Ever Private Satellite." Science Alert. Last modified October 28, 2016. Accessed November 29, 2016. http://www.sciencealert .com/14-awesome-teenage-girls-have-built-africa-s-first-ever-private-satellite.

Medel, Shana. "Florida Teen Creates Company to Give Teddy Bears to Fallen Officers' Families." *Orlando Sentinel*. Last modified February 21, 2017. Accessed May 16, 2017. http://www.orlandosentinel .com/features/os-blue-line-bears-honor-fallen-officers-20170221-story.html.

Meur, Hannah. *Pixel Crochet: 101 Supercool 8-bit Inspired Designs to Crochet*. New York: Lark Books, 2015.

Miller, Kimberly D., Stuart J. Schleien, Brooke Paula, Frisoli M. Antoniette, and Wade T. Brooks, III. "Community for All: The Therapeutic Recreation Practitioner's Role in Inclusive Volunteering." *Therapeutic Recreation Journal* 39, no. 1 (First Quarter 2005): 18–31. ProQuest.

Miller, Kimberly D., Stuart J. Schleien, Cecilia Rider, Crystal Hall, Megan Roche, and James Worsley. "Inclusive Volunteering: Benefits to Participants and Community." *Therapeutic Recreation Journal* 36, no. 3 (Third Quarter 2002). ProQuest.

Mycoskie, Blake. *Start Something That Matters*. 2012 ed. New York: Spiegel & Grau, 2012.

Nelson, Judith A., and Daniel Eckstein. "A Service-Learning Model for at-Risk Adolescents." *Education and Treatment of Children* 31, no. 2 (2008): 223–37. http://jerome.stjohns.edu:81/login?url=https:// search-proquest-com.jerome.stjohns.edu/docview/202675510?accountid=14068.

NY1 News. "'Little Free Library' Opens in St. George NYPD Precinct." Spectrum News NY 1. Last modified January 3, 2016. Accessed May 16, 2017. http://www.ny1.com/nyc/staten-island/ news/2016/01/3/-little-free-library-opens-in-st-george-nypd-precinct.html.

NYLC. *K-12 Service-Learning Standards for Quality Practice*. St. Paul, MN: National Youth Leadership Council, 2009.

O'Connor, Michael P. "Service Works! Promoting Transition Success for Students with Disabilities through Participation in Service Learning." *Teaching Exceptional Children* 41, no. 6 (July/August 2009): 13–17. Academic Search Premier.

Pittman, Taylor. "Meet the 6-Year-Old Fighting Vandals of Jewish Cemeteries with Kindness." *The Huffington Post*. Last modified April 5, 2017. Accessed April 8, 2017. http://www.huffingtonpost .com/entry/meet-the-6-year-old-fighting-vandals-of-jewish-cemeteries-with-kindness_us_58e534f-de4b06a4cb30e86f2?

Price-Mitchell, Mariln. "Community Service Ideas for Youth: Why Giving Back Matters." Roots of Action. Last modified May 26, 2015. Accessed May 12, 2016. http://www.rootsofaction.com/ community-service-ideas-for-youth/.

Purdue University. "EPICS High School Project Examples." EPICS. Accessed December 30, 2016. http://eng.purdue.edu/jump/c8a05c.

Purdue University. "What Is EPICS?" EPICS. Accessed December 30, 2016. https://engineering.purdue .edu/EPICS/k12/about/what-is-epics.

Rabea, Malik, and Rose Pauline. *Financing Education in Pakistan—Opportunities for Action, Country Case Study for the Oslo Summit on Education for Development*. N.p.: n.p., 2015. Accessed November 11, 2016. http://www.academia.edu/15327837/Financing_Education_in_Pakistan_-_Opportunities_ for_Action_Country_Case_Study_for_the_Oslo_Summit_on_Education_for_Development_.

"The Rachel Project." International Association of Bomb Technicians and Investigators. Accessed April 17, 2017. https://www.iabti.org/charity/category/news.

Rice, Francesca. "People Are Crocheting Octopuses to Help Premature Babies." Prima. Last modified January 23, 2017. Accessed March 6, 2017. http://www.prima.co.uk/family/kids/news/a37423/ crocheted-octopuses-help-premature-babies/.

Rose, Deborah Lee, and Jane Veltkamp. *Beauty and the Beak: How Science, Technology and a 3D Printed Beak Rescued a Bald Eagle*. Apex, NC: Persnickety Press, 2017.

Russell, Natalie M. "Teaching More Than English: Connecting ESL Students to Their Community through Services Learning." *Phi Delta Kappan* 88, no. 10 (June 1, 2017): 770–71. Academic Search Premier.

Shaar, Deborah. "A New Type of Food Pantry Is Sprouting in Yards across America." NPR. Last modified January 11, 2017. Accessed January 11, 2017. http://www.npr.org/sections/thesalt/2017/01/11/508931473/a-new-type-of-food-pantry-is-sprouting-in-yards-across-america.

Simmons, Ann M. "The World's Trash Crisis, and Why Many Americans Are Oblivious." *Los Angeles Times*, April 22, 2016. Accessed January 18, 2017. http://www.latimes.com/world/global-development/la-fg-global-trash-20160422-20160421-snap-htmlstory.html.

Sims, Jade. *Craft Hope: Handmade Crafts for a Cause*. New York: Lark Crafts, 2010.

Spring, Kimberly, Nathan Dietz, and Robert Grimm Jr. *Building Active Citizens: The Role of Social Institutions in Teen Volunteering*. Brief no. 3. March 2007. Accessed November 28, 2016. http://www.nationalservice.gov/pdf/07_0406_disad_youth.pdf.

Spring, Kimberly, Nathan Dietz, and Robert Grimm, Jr. *Educating for Active Citizenship: Service-Learning, School-Based Service, and Civic Engagement*. Brief no. 2. March 2006. Accessed November 28, 2016. http://www.nationalservice.gov/pdf/06_0323_SL_briefing.pdf.

Thompson, Laurie Ann. *Be a Changemaker: How to Start Something That Matters*. New York: Simon Pulse, 2014.

"Undernutrition Contributes to Nearly Half of All Deaths in Children under 5 and Is Widespread in Asia and Africa." UNICEF. Last modified September 2016. Accessed November 10, 2016. http://data.unicef.org/topic/nutrition/malnutrition/.

UNICEF. *The State of the World's Children 2016: A Fair Chance for Every Child*. June 2016. Accessed November 11, 2016. https://www.unicef.org/sowc2016/.

United States Interagency Council on Homelessness. *Opening Doors: Federal Strategic Plan to Prevent and End Homelessness*. June 2015. Accessed November 29, 2016. https://www.usich.gov/resources/uploads/asset_library/USICH_OpeningDoors_Amendment2015_FINAL.pdf.

University of Colorado Boulder. "Picture Books for Visually Impaired Kids Go 3D Thanks to CU-Boulder Research Team." *CU Boulder Today*. Last modified June 23, 2014. Accessed April 3, 2017. http://www.colorado.edu/today/2014/06/23/picture-books-visually-impaired-kids-go-3d-thanks-cu-boulder-research-team.

U.S. Environmental Protection Agency. "Reduce Waste." A Student's Guide to Global Climate Change. Last modified March 3, 2016. Accessed January 18, 2017. https://www3.epa.gov/climatechange/kids/solutions/actions/waste.html.

"Why Youth Service?" Youth Service America. Accessed November 5, 2016. http://ysa.org/about/why-youth-service/.

Wu, Huiting. *Social Impact of Volunteerism*. August 30, 2011. Accessed July 15, 2017. http://www.pointsoflight.org/sites/default/files/site-content/files/social_impact_of_volunteerism_pdf.pdf.

"Young Artists Create Soothing Images for Patients." WellSpan Health. Last modified March 28, 2016. Accessed November 20, 2016. https://www.wellspan.org/news/story/16130.

Yousafzai, Malala. "We Can Finally Give the World's Poorest Children the Education They Deserve." Editorial. *The Guardian*, June 24, 2014. Accessed November 11, 2016. https://www.theguardian.com/commentisfree/2014/jun/24/worlds-poorest-children-education-global-partnership.

"YSA About." Youth Service America. Accessed November 5, 2016. http://ysa.org/about/.

Index

About the Author

GINA SEYMOUR is library media specialist at Islip High School on Long Island, New York, and is adjunct professor at St. John's University, Queens, New York. She received the Library Journal Mover & Shaker Change Agent award in 2017 and was awarded the Suffolk School Library Media Association's School Librarian of the Year in 2014. She is an active speaker and presenter on the maker movement, compassionate making, and inclusive makerspaces on a national level. Her MakerCare program has garnered national attention and has served as an inspiration for libraries across the country. Gina shares her work, musings, and reflections on her blog GinaSeymour.com and on Twitter @ginaseymour.